KU-607-635

# Foreword

PRACTICAL FIRST AID began its life as an excellent account of the elements of first aid, written for Youth and Junior members of the British Red Cross Society by that doyen of first aid instructors, Dr. A. S. Playfair. It proved to be so popular that, in subsequent editions, its scope was widened to include a readership of adults interested in learning about the basic skills of first aid.

This edition aims to embrace a similar readership, extending to those who are designated Appointed Persons under the current Health and Safety Regulations; it is hoped, also, that holders of the Standard First Aid Certificate may find it useful, to carry in a rucksack, keep at home or with a first aid kit, for quick reference when an aide-memoire is needed on being confronted with a particular emergency for the first time.

The style has changed to accord with modern tastes. In content, some old hands may be disappointed to find no direct reference to compression of the brain but it is a personal view that there is nothing to be gained by cluttering the mind with descriptions of conditions which the first aider can do nothing to alleviate and which might distract him or her from the prime duty — which is to ensure a clear airway whilst getting every unconscious casualty to hospital as quickly as possible. Cardio-pulmonary resuscitation for infants has also been omitted because it is considered that the extreme delicacy of skill needed safely to apply mouth-to-mouth or external chest compression techniques to infants is beyond that which is expected of someone taking the first steps in first aid. In any case, when compared with the much more common instances of choking, or simple breath-holding (which gain mention), causes of cardiac or respiratory arrest in infants which might benefit from the ministrations of first aiders are extremely rare.

Mouth-to-mouth ventilation is now known to be more than twice as effective as manual methods; the Holger Nielsen method has been described in the appendix, to be used only on those rare occasions when it may prove physically impossible to use the preferred method.

This is a practical manual for beginners. It describes what to do in any emergency with only the essential descriptions needed for understanding as to why one does it; and it is written in language which, it is hoped, will be readily understood by readers who are not familiar with the jargon used by doctors and nurses. Those who wish to advance further are strongly recommended to take a course in *Standard First Aid* for which the approved text is the First Aid Manual of the three Voluntary Aid Societies.

## Acknowledgments

The compilation of this book has been a team effort. The whole project was master-minded, from the outset, by Director of Marketing Services of The British Red Cross Society, Mr J. M. Jerram. The Director of Training, Miss Margaret Baker, and Mr Jim Williams, have — in addition to technical advice — given invaluable guidance on what learners, with no previous knowledge of first aid, might be expected to understand and accept. I am grateful, also, to Mr E. A. Malkin, FRCS, for reading and correcting proofs and for much sage advice.

Finally, the Society must acknowledge its debt to the Publishers, Dorling Kindersley, who — in this, as in other publications, have brought an entirely fresh approach to the instruction of what might otherwise seem prosaic or, even, unattractive subjects. In particular I would like to express my gratitude to Miss Jemima Dunne for painstaking editing and patient re-writing of submitted prose, to make it intelligible to the uninitiated reader. Our thanks, also, go to the team of illustrators, and the models, who have worked so hard to make this manual attractive as well as instructive.

Brigadier D. D. O'Brien MB B.Ch BAO
Chief Medical Officer
*The British Red Cross Society*

# Principles of first aid

## What is first aid?

First aid is the first assistance or treatment given to a casualty before the arrival of an ambulance or qualified expert.

## The object of first aid is to:

- preserve life
- prevent the injury or condition becoming worse
- promote recovery.

## The first aider's task is to:

- find out what happened without endangering him or herself
- reassure and protect the person from any further danger
- deal with the injury or condition as required
- arrange for travel home or to a hospital as necessary.

## What equipment is needed?

You do not need any special equipment. First aid kits do contain many useful items such as bandages and dressings but a good first aider does not depend on them. You should use whatever you have readily available and improvise if necessary.

# How to handle an accident

After any accident involving casualties it is essential that you remain calm and confident while you assess the situation and carry out treatment; this will reassure the casualties and convince bystanders of your ability to cope.

We have used a street incident to illustrate some of the complications you may encounter; however, the same principles apply to any accident whether at home, at work or on the road. Use your common sense, know your limitations and do not attempt to do too much.

**1** Look around you. Make sure you take in everything: for example, casualties may have been thrown some distance from the car, even over a hedge.

**2** Check that the casualty is not exposed to any further danger such as fire, gas, electricity, on-coming traffic, or crumbling buildings, for example. If there is anything, remove the danger from the casualty and only if this is not possible, remove the casualty from the danger.

**3** Quickly decide which casualty is the most seriously injured and treat him or her first according to the priorities listed right.

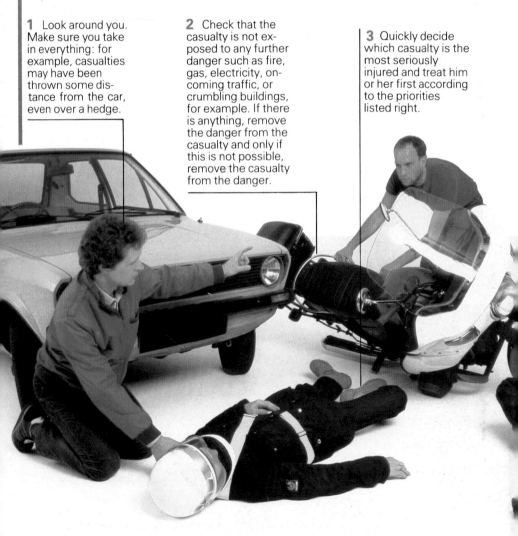

# IMPORTANT

**Make sure that by approaching any incident or casualty you are not putting your own life at risk.**

**Never touch any casualty while he or she is still in contact with electricity or you risk being electrocuted yourself. Follow the procedure described on page 8.**

**Never let anyone smoke near a crashed car; there may be petrol, oil or chemicals on the road.**

**4** Send for an ambulance or doctor as required, giving accurate details (see page 9).

**+** Points to look for to help you find out what is wrong.
● **History**, how did it happen (ask both casualties and by-standers)?
● **Symptoms**, what does the casualty feel and tell you (for example, pain, inability to move or feel a limb)?
● **Signs**, what can you see and feel on gentle examination (for example, level of consciousness, bleeding, weak pulse, deformed limbs, change in skin colour)? Look for medical warning signs such as *Medic-alert bracelets*.

# Priorities

The priorities for treatment of any casualty are listed below. However, in all incidents where there are several casualties, the most severely injured must always be treated first but remember, the noisy casualty may not be the most seriously injured.

**1** A B C must be established within three minutes if the casualty is unconscious in order to prevent permanent injury.

**A** The *Airway* (the passage between the mouth, nose and throat) must be opened and kept open if the casualty is unconscious or choking (see pages 12 to 15).

**B** *Breathing* must be established and maintained (see pages 10 and 12 to 14).

**C** *Circulation* of blood must be maintained (see pages 16 to 17).

**2** *Severe bleeding* must be stopped immediately (see page 23).

**3** *Broken bones* must be immobilised if the casualty is to be moved (see pages 46 to 55). Do not move a casualty with a suspected spine injury; treat as on page 49.

**4** Reassure the casualty and treat any other injuries as required.

# Additional hazards

It is important after any incident that by attempting to help an injured person you do not become a casualty yourself. Some incidents are particularly dangerous because the casualty may still be in contact with electricity, near a fire or in a road accident involving a vehicle carrying dangerous chemicals. In any of these situations, you must take the following precautions.

### Electrical injuries

If the casualty is still in contact with electricity, STOP THE CURRENT at once by switching it off at the mains or pulling out the plug. If this is not possible, knock the casualty's limb clear of the electrical contact. Stand on a dry surface, for example, a piece of wood, a folded newspaper or a rubber mat, and carefully knock the limb clear using a similar material as shown below. Avoid touching anything wet because water conducts elecricity. *Do not attempt first aid until the contact has been broken.*

## IMPORTANT

**Electricity from overhead cables or from some factory installations is far more powerful than home electricity. If a casualty is touching, or near, these cables, it is impossible to give first aid and *very* dangerous to approach the casualty before the current has been stopped. *Remain at least 20m (20yd) away from the casualty and call the police.***

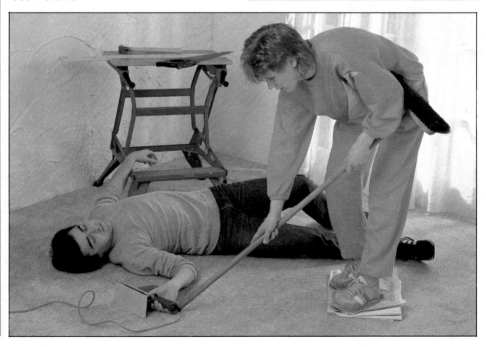

## Dangerous chemicals

Vans and lorries carrying dangerous chemicals can be involved in road accidents. These vehicles now have to display panels which indicate the chemical they are carrying, its properties, a special code number and a telephone number. If you come across one of these signs, *do not approach the vehicle*; note the details on the panel and give them to the emergency services.

Poisonous substances

Substances liable to ignite spontaneously

Flammable substances

Radioactive substances

Compressed gases

Corrosive substances

**2YE**
**1089**
Newtown-on-Moors
(0123) 45678

Denotes that a vehicle is carrying an oxidising agent.

### Fire

If you are confronted by a fire at home or in the street, act quickly and precisely. Call the emergency services, giving as much detail as possible. *Do not enter a burning room or building* alone and you must have, and know how to use, breathing apparatus. Not only is there a danger of your being overcome by smoke, but also fire spreads very quickly and you may be burnt yourself. Moreover, a great deal of modern furniture is made of materials that give off poisonous fumes when burning; these fumes can kill in a matter of seconds.

# Calling for help

Throughout this book we recommend that you refer the casualty to medical aid if you are in any doubt about the condition. Medical aid means treatment by a doctor at a hospital or surgery.

Ambulances are normally needed to take a casualty to hospital from *all* serious outdoor accidents and *any* incident involving: difficulty in breathing, heart failure, severe bleeding, unconsciousness, serious burns, suspected fractures (although casualties with arm fractures can usually be taken to hospital by car), shock or poisoning.

### Calling the emergency services

If possible always stay with a casualty and send a reliable bystander to the nearest telephone with instructions to:
- dial 999 and ask for the appropriate emergency services (normally ambulance because each switchboard has access to all the others)
- give the telephone number in case for any reason he or she is cut off
- give details of: the exact location of the incident describing any landmarks that may help the ambulance driver to find it, what happened and the suspected cause, the number and approximate age of any casualties involved and the extent of the injuries
- replace the receiver *after* and not before the ambulance control officer does so
- come back and tell you that the call has been made.

# Breathing

Every part of the body uses oxygen for life and energy and the brain uses more than any other part. Breathing is the process by which oxygen is taken into the lungs and carbon dioxide, a waste product, is expelled from the body.

　　Air contains oxygen so each time we breathe in we take oxygen into our lungs. The oxygen is then picked up by the blood and carried through the circulatory system to all parts of the body (see page 24). In the body tissues the oxygen is given up by the blood, and the carbon dioxide is picked up and brought back to the lungs.

*Asphyxia* occurs if there is not enough oxygen available to the tissues. It can result from:
- inadequate oxygen content in the air as occurs in a smoke-filled room
- obstruction of the air passages – nose, mouth, throat or windpipe – for example, choking (see page 20)
- interference with, or paralysis of, the muscle action in the chest, for example when a person is buried in sand or following electrocution.

　　Finally, adequate blood circulation (see pages 18 and 24) is needed to get the oxygen to the tissues.

**A**　**Airway** *Open the casualty's airway* (see page 13) to allow unobstructed passage of fresh air to the casualty's lungs.

**B**　Check **Breathing** Place your ear next to the casualty's mouth and nose to *Check breathing* (see page 13). If necessary, begin *Artificial ventilation* (see page 14 to 15) to get air into the lungs.

**C**　Check **Circulation** If necessary, apply *External chest compression* (see page 16 to 17) to apply pressure to the chest and so pump blood through the arteries to the vital organs.

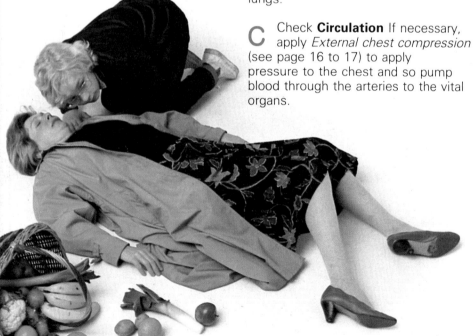

# How we breathe

By using the muscles between our ribs and the diaphragm (a dome-shaped muscle which separates the chest from the lower part of the trunk) to expand our chests we draw air into our LUNGS. The air enters the body through the nose and mouth then passes into the WINDPIPE (trachea), the tube that goes down the neck and into the chest. This tube divides into two TUBES (bronchi), one for each lung. These tubes then subdivide into hundreds of smaller ones, each of which ends in a micro-scopic AIR SAC. This collection of air sacs forms the bulk of the lungs and it is here that the exchange of gases takes place: carbon dioxide is given up by the blood and oxygen is taken up.

To breathe out, the muscles relax, the chest falls back into the resting position, compressing the lungs and sending used air back up through the windpipe and out of the body.

Normally, we breathe in and out about 16 times per minute. The rate is faster in babies and small children and it is increased during exercise and in some disorders. Calculate a person's breathing rate by counting the number of times the chest rises in a minute.

**Respiratory system**

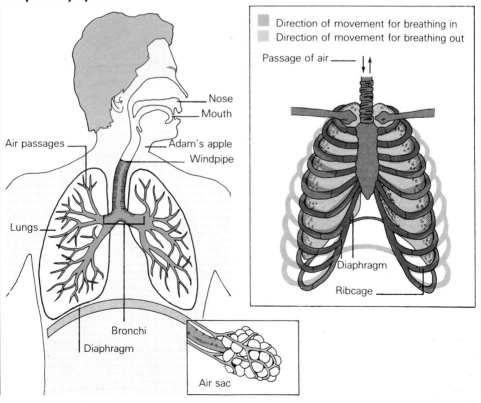

- Nose
- Mouth
- Air passages
- Adam's apple
- Windpipe
- Lungs
- Bronchi
- Diaphragm
- Air sac

Direction of movement for breathing in
Direction of movement for breathing out
Passage of air
Diaphragm
Ribcage

# Resuscitation

When a casualty has stopped breathing you must immediately try to revive him or her by getting air into the lungs. This procedure is known as artificial ventilation or "rescue breathing". It cannot be stressed enough that in this emergency, NO TIME CAN BE WASTED. A casualty rescued from drowning who is not breathing, for instance, must be given artificial ventilation as soon as his or her head is free from the water; do not wait until the casualty is ashore.

Remember the priorities ABC from page 7. First you must position the head as described opposite — if the tongue has been blocking the airway, the casualty may begin breathing immediately. If the casualty does not begin breathing, clear the airway, see far right. If there is still no breathing, begin *mouth-to-mouth ventilation* — the "kiss of life" (see page 14). This involves breathing air from your lungs into the casualty's mouth (or nose) and it is possible because you use only about a quarter of the oxygen you breathe in; the rest is breathed out.

If mouth-to-mouth is impossible because for example, the casualty is trapped face down, then you can use Holger Nielsen, a manual method of ventilation (see page 92).

# The airway

When a healthy, conscious person is breathing there is plenty of space for air to move from the nose and mouth to the windpipe. If a casualty is unconscious this space may be narrowed or blocked for several reasons: the tongue may fall back and block the airway; the head may have tilted forward narrowing the top of the windpipe; or vomit may be lying in the back of the air passage unable to drain away. Whatever the reason, the result is that breathing is difficult or impossible because air cannot get through.

**Healthy, conscious person asleep**      **Unconscious casualty**

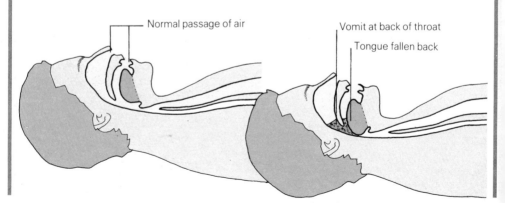

Normal passage of air

Vomit at back of throat

Tongue fallen back

# Opening the airway

If a casualty is unconscious and particularly if she is lying face up, air cannot get into the lungs because the airway may be narrowed or blocked. So, it is very important to first *open the airway by tilting the head right back with the lower jaw lifted well forward.*

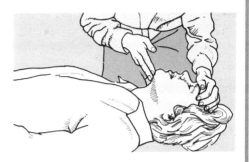

## IMPORTANT

**If you suspect a fractured neck (see page 49), do not tilt or turn the head, simply pull the lower jaw forward.**

Lift the chin forward with the index and middle fingers of one hand while pressing her forehead backwards with the heel of your other hand.

# Checking breathing

To find out whether an unconscious person is breathing, *look, listen* and *feel*.

**1** Place your ear close to the casualty's mouth and look along her chest. If she is breathing you can see the chest moving and hear and feel the breaths.

**2** If the casualty is breathing, place her in the *recovery position* (see page 18).

# Clearing the airway

If the casualty is not breathing after the airway has been opened, it may still be blocked – by broken teeth, mud or vomit. Keeping the casualty's head well back, turn it to one side and with one quick sweep around the mouth with two fingers lift out any foreign matter. Make sure that you do not push it any further down. Do not turn the head if you suspect a fractured neck.

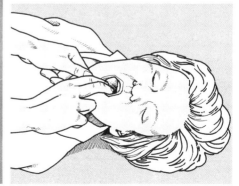

# Mouth~to~mouth ventilation

The following instructions are for giving mouth-to-mouth to unconscious adults who are not breathing. At first this may seem a complicated series of steps but with practice you will find that it is quite straightforward.

You should not attempt mouth-to-mouth until you have been taught how to do it by a trained instructor and you should never practise it on a person who is breathing normally.

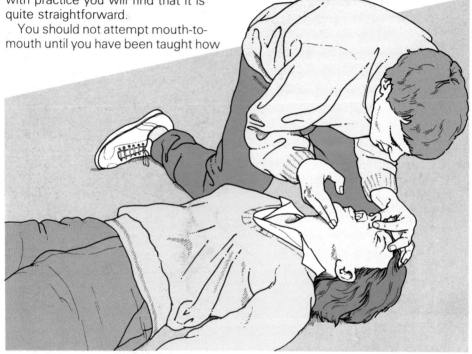

**1** Open and, if necessary, clear the casualty's airway. Keeping her head well back, her jaw lifted and the mouth open, pinch her nostrils shut with the fingers and thumb of one hand; *maintain this position throughout.*

**2** Take a deep breath, open your mouth wide and seal your lips around the casualty's mouth.

**3** Blow firmly but gently into the casualty's mouth; blow from your chest not your cheeks and blow hard enough to make her chest rise.

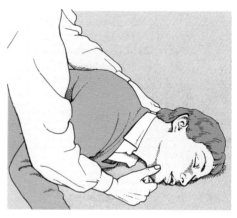

**4** Kneel beside the casualty, about 22.5cm (9in) from his chest and support his head with one hand. Grasp the casualty's clothes at the hip farthest from you and pull him towards you until he is resting against your knees.

**5** Re-adjust the casualty's head so that it is now well back to make sure the airway stays open.

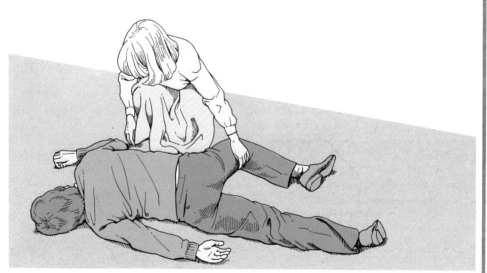

**6** Working on the uppermost limbs, bend first the arm, then the leg into a convenient position to prevent the casualty rolling on to his face.

**7** The arm behind the casualty should now be free. If it is not, carefully ease it out from under his back and leave it lying parallel to his body to prevent him rolling on to his back.

# Choking

This is the result of a blockage of the windpipe. It can happen if food or vomit goes "down the wrong way" or if something like a broken tooth or denture were to slip down the back of the throat.

## Symptoms and signs
● the casualty suddenly brings her hand to the throat and is unable to speak
● if not relieved, the casualty may turn blue in the face and the veins in the face and neck will begin to stand out
● if the blockage is still not removed, the casualty will lose consciousness.

## Action

**1** Ask the person if she can cough; if she can, encourage her to do so and do not interfere.

**2** Tell the casualty to bend forward so that her head is lower than her chest. If she cannot cough, give her four sharp slaps between the shoulder blades with the heel of your hand. Repeat these back slaps up to four times if necessary.

**3** Check inside the casualty's mouth. The casualty can run her finger around the back of her mouth and try to hook out any foreign matter she finds; be prepared to do it for her if it becomes necessary.

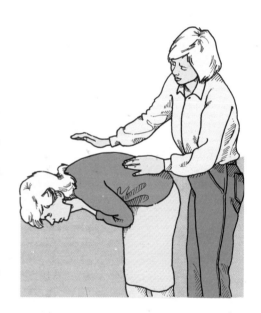

## Small children and infants

If the casualty is a baby or small child, give back slaps but use less force.

**Small child**
Kneel down and lay him or her across your thigh with the head down and give four quick slaps between the shoulders.

**Infant** (see *right*)
Lay the baby along your forearm so that she is face down and her head is below her chest. Support the head and shoulders with one hand and give her four light slaps on her back with the other hand.

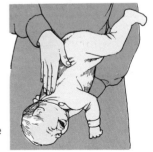

# Suffocation

This occurs when air is prevented from entering a person's mouth or nose, for example when an unconscious casualty's tongue falls back and blocks the airway (see page 13); there is a pillow or plastic bag over a person's mouth; a person is drowning; a casualty is buried under a fall of earth or sand.

Suffocation will also result when the air that enters the airway is polluted with smoke or poisonous gas for example, exhaust fumes, which prevent oxygen being absorbed in the lungs by the blood.

## Symptoms and signs

- difficulty in breathing; breathing appears laboured and fast
- snoring or gurgling sounds while trying to breathe
- frothing at the mouth
- lips and fingernails will become blue.

## Action

**1** Immediately remove the cause of obstruction from the face or neck or remove the casualty from the danger area without endangering yourself. Then *open the airway* (see page 13).

**4** As a last resort, if the casualty is still not breathing, stand behind her, clench your fist and place it over her stomach (upper abdomen). Grasp your fist with your other hand (see inset) then pull suddenly inward and upward; the obstruction will often shoot into and out of the mouth.

**5** If the casualty loses consciousness, *open and clear the airway* (see page 13) and begin *mouth-to-mouth* (see page 14).

**2** If the casualty is buried under a pile of earth or sand, remove it as far back as the hips so that the chest can expand during breathing.

**3** If the casualty does not breathe after the airway has been opened, begin *mouth-to-mouth* immediately (see page 14).

**4** Seek medical aid.

# Wounds and bleeding

A *wound* is an injury which breaks the skin or other tissues and which can allow blood to escape from the body and germs to enter it (see page 26).

*Bleeding* occurs when any of the vessels that carry blood around the body, arteries, veins or capillaries, are cut or torn (see *Blood circulation*, page 24). It may be external, therefore visible, or internal and invisible. Blood from an artery (*arterial bleeding*) is bright red and spurts from a wound in time with the heartbeat, and blood from a vein (*venous bleeding*) is darker red and pours or gushes. Blood from the capillaries is medium red and oozes from a wound.

Serious blood loss is always an emergency and must be controlled as soon as possible. If a large amount of blood is lost, *shock* and eventually death can result (see page 25).

Bleeding stops when a clot or "plug" forms in the wound. You can help by pressing directly on to the wound to flatten the surrounding blood vessels (*direct pressure*) and by raising the injured part (*elevation*) which reduces the blood flow in the area.

For serious external bleeding follow the steps described opposite; for small cuts and grazes, see page 26. Treatment for any bleeding that requires special action is on pages 28 to 33.

## Symptoms and signs

Although blood is usually the most obvious sign of a wound there are a number of other possibilities to look out for indicated in the captions around this photograph.

**+Symptoms and signs of shock**
This is a serious condition which will develop if blood loss is severe and prolonged (see page 25).

**+ Blood**
Look for evidence of severe external blood loss on the casualty's clothes.

**+ Danger**
Make sure that the casualty is not in any further danger (for example, lying on broken glass).

**✚ Cause of injury**
There may be
something near the
casualty which in-
dicates the cause of
injury (for example,
broken glass from a
window).

**✚ Foreign body**
If a foreign body,
for example a piece
of glass, is stuck in
a wound *do not
remove it*. It may
be plugging the
wound preventing
bleeding and you
could make the in-
jury worse when
you remove it.
Treat as described
on page 28.

## Action

**1** Apply *direct pressure* by pressing
over the wound with your thumb
and/or fingers – preferably over a clean
pad. You may need to maintain
pressure for up to ten minutes.

**2** Raise and support the injured part
so that it is above the heart (chest).

**3** Place a *sterile dressing* (see
page 27) over the wound so that
it extends well beyond the area of
the wound, and secure it firmly with
the attached bandage. If there is no
dressing available, improvise (see
*Emergency dressings* page 27).

**4** If blood begins to show through
the dressing, *do not* remove it
but put more dressings on top of the
original one and bandage firmly.

**5** Watch for any symptoms
and signs of *shock* and treat
accordingly (see page 25).

# Blood circulation

Blood consists of cells suspended in a fluid called *plasma*. It is pumped from the heart through arteries to every part of the body and returns to the heart in veins. It carries oxygen (from the lungs, see page 11), nourishment (from digested food) and warmth to the body tissues and waste matter away.

Very simply the circulation works as follows. The LEFT side of the HEART pumps bright red blood loaded with oxygen into the main artery (AORTA). This then subdivides into smaller and smaller ARTERIES going to all parts of the body. Eventually each small artery divides into a network of microscopic tubes with very thin walls called CAPILLARIES. The nourishment and the oxygen carried in the blood are passed through these walls into the tissues and any waste (including carbon dioxide) is picked up by the blood.

The capillaries then join up to form small VEINS which carry the blood, now dark red because it contains no oxygen, back to the heart. Veins from all over the body join up to form two large veins which empty into the RIGHT

**The circulatory system**

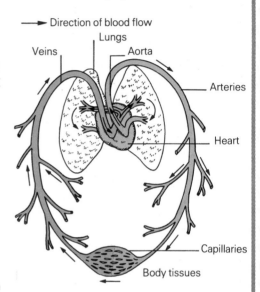

→ Direction of blood flow
Lungs
Veins
Aorta
Arteries
Heart
Capillaries
Body tissues

side of the HEART.

The heart pumps this blood up to the lungs where the carbon dioxide is lost and a new supply of oxygen is taken up. Refreshed with oxygen and bright red again, the blood returns to the left side of the heart and the cycle continues.

## Pulse

This is a throb which passes along every artery with each beat of the heart. It can be felt when the artery lies close to the surface, for example at the wrist (*radial pulse*) or at the neck (see page 18).

To practise finding the radial pulse, place the pads of three fingers in the hollow immediately above the creases on the front of your wrist in line with the thumb pad and press firmly. Count the number of beats in a minute and note the rate, strength and rhythm. A normal pulse is regular and strong. In adults the heart beats 60–80 times a minute; in children it beats up to 100 times.

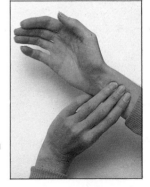

# Shock

This is a condition in which the blood circulation, which supplies oxygen to the tissues, fails. There are many possible causes and they fall into two main groups. Firstly, the heart may become weak so the pressure of the circulating blood falls, or the heart beat may stop altogether. Secondly, the amount of blood in circulation may become reduced so that there is not enough left to supply all the body cells with oxygen. This can result from external bleeding (see page 22), internal bleeding (see below) or loss of body fluids following widespread burns, severe vomiting or diarrhoea or a severe allergic reaction.

## Action

**1** Stop external bleeding as soon as possible (see page 23).

**2** Reassure the casualty and move her as little as possible. Lay her down and shelter her from any extremes of temperature turn her head to one side.

**3** Raise her legs by putting folded coats under her feet. Loosen her collar and any tight clothing.

**4** Keep the casualty comfortably warm.

**5** Send a bystander for an ambulance or medical aid.

## Symptoms and signs
- casualty becomes very pale and grey (this is most obvious inside the lips)
- skin is cold and moist with sweat
- pulse will be weak and rapid
- breathing is shallow and fast
- she may become restless and begin yawning and sighing (air hunger)
- she may be thirsty
- finally, she may lose consciousness and die if treatment is not successful.

## IMPORTANT
**Do not give the casualty anything to eat or drink.**

**Never use a hot water bottle to warm the casualty.**

## Internal bleeding

This can result from an injury causing a major bone, such as the pelvis, to break or causing damage to an internal organ or from some illness which causes sudden severe bleeding inside the body cavity.

Suspect internal bleeding if you notice an unusually large degree of swelling around the injured part, if the casualty complains of sudden severe pains in the chest or abdomen, or if the symptoms and signs of shock develop rapidly, see above.

# Small cuts and grazes

Any break in the skin, however small, can allow germs (bacteria) to enter the body. Germs are micro-organisms carried, for example, by flies or un-washed hands; if allowed to settle in a wound, they grow and cause infection.

## Action

*You will need*:
- dressing (see opposite)
- soap and water
- cotton wool and gauze swabs or antiseptic wipes if available.

**1** Sit the casualty down and tem-porarily protect the wound by covering it with a clean piece of gauze or paper tissue. Wash your hands.

**2** Collect the required equipment, see above, and place it on a piece of clean, disposable material. Never cough over the wound or equipment.

**3** If the wound is dirty, lightly rinse it under cold running water until clean. Then gently clean around it with soap and water. Do this with the cotton wool or gauze swabs or antiseptic wipes; always work from the wound outwards and use a fresh swab for each stroke. Be careful not to disturb any blood clots as this may start the bleeding again.

With small cuts and grazes the bleeding soon stops of its own accord.

The aim of treatment for this type of injury therefore is to clean and dress the wound as soon as possible to minimise infection.

**4** Carefully remove any *loose* foreign matter such as glass, metal or gravel (see *Small foreign bodies* page 82).

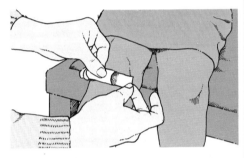

**5** Dry the area around the wound and dress the wound. If the wound is small, place an *adhesive dressing* over the area. If it is larger, apply a *sterile dressing* (see opposite) or a piece of gauze and a pad of cotton wool over it. Secure it with a bandage.

**6** Rest the injured part.

## IMPORTANT

**Never dress a wound with cotton wool or anything fluffy.**

# Dressings

There are two main types of dressing: *sterile dressings*, which should always be used for large or serious wounds if available; and *adhesive dressings*, commonly used for small cuts and grazes. Whichever dressing you use, always make sure that the pad extends well beyond the area of the wound.

### Sterile dressing

This is a dressing which consists of layers of gauze and a pad of cotton wool attached to a roller bandage. Each dressing is sterilised and sealed in a protective wrapping.

To apply a sterile dressing, hold the edge of the folded dressing and the main rolled bandage in one hand and unfold the short bandage. Place the pad, gauze-side down, on the wound. Do not touch the pad, although, if necessary, guide it by placing your fingers along the edge of the pad as you put it over the wound. Wind the short end of the bandage once around the limb to secure the dressing (A). Then, leaving the short end hanging, bandage firmly with the rolled end. Tie the ends together over the pad (B) using a *reef knot* (see page 41).

A

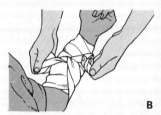

B

Sterile dressings

Adhesive dressings

### Adhesive dressing

Often called a plaster, this consists of a small pad attached to an adhesive backing. Each dressing is supplied sealed in an individual packet. The surrounding skin must be completely dry before you use this dressing.

### Emergency dressings

If you have no dressings, use any clean *non-fluffy* material such as a handkerchief, paper tissue or pillow case instead.

Wash your hands, then hold the material by the corners and let it fall open. Refold it to the size you need so that what was the inside, un-exposed surface, is now on the outside. Handle the dressing by the edges and corners only and do not let the clean surface touch anything before putting it on the wound.

# Embedded objects in wounds

Do not remove any object that appears to be stuck or embedded in a wound. Firstly, because it may be plugging the wound preventing bleeding and secondly because you may do more damage by pulling it out. Instead you should protect the wound and the object with gauze and place a built-up dressing made of pads of cotton wool held in place with a bandage around the object. This helps maintain enough pressure to control bleeding without pressing directly on the wound or the projecting object.

## Action

**1** Control severe bleeding by pressing the area immediately above and below the object.

**2** Help the casualty lie down and raise and support the injured part. Drape a piece of gauze over the wound and object.

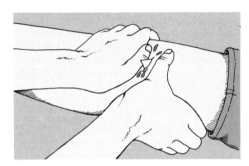

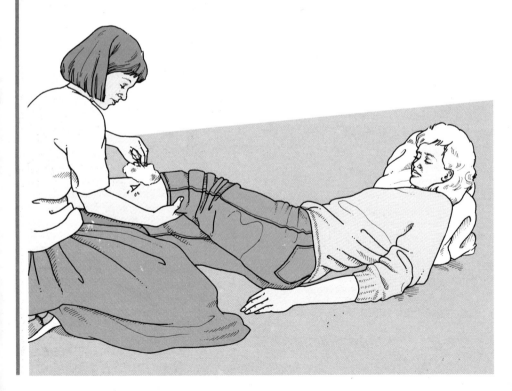

**3** Very carefully build up pads of
cotton wool around the object
until they are at least the same height
as the object. Do not pull the gauze
down as you do this. If it is not possible
to build up the dressing high enough,
leave the embedded object protruding.

**4** Place the end of a roller bandage
over the part of the built-up
dressing nearest you and make two
straight turns around the limb.

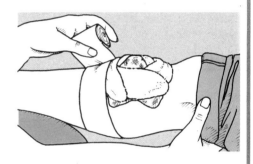

**5** Pass the bandage under the limb
and bring it up over the upper
edge of the dressing.

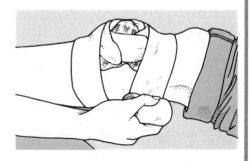

**6** Continue making these diagonal
turns until the dressing is firm,
then secure the bandage (see page 68).

**7** Keeping the injured part raised,
immobilise the limb as for a
broken bone (see pages 46 to 57).

**8** Transfer the casualty to hospital.

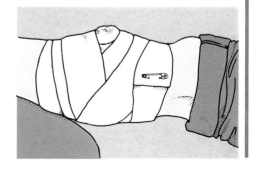

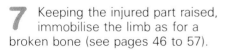

# Bleeding from the palm of the hand

This type of injury will bleed a great deal and it is often difficult to apply enough pressure to control it. Bandage as described below provided you are sure that there is nothing embedded in the wound. If there is, see page 28.

## Action

**1** Sit or lay the casualty down and raise his arm above the level of his chest. Press on the wound with your thumb to control bleeding.

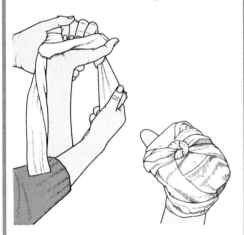

**2** Cover the wound with a sterile dressing and ask the casualty to clench his fist tightly over the pad (top); you may have to help him. Leaving the short end free, wind the bandage around the fist. Tie the ends in a *reef knot* (see page 41) across the top of his knuckles to help maintain pressure.

**3** Support his arm in an *elevation sling* (see page 56).

**4** Seek medical aid.

# Bleeding from a tooth socket

This may happen immediately after accidental loss of a tooth or some considerable time after a tooth has been removed by a dentist.

## Action

**1** Sit the casualty down and incline the head towards the injured side.

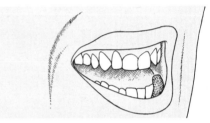

**2** Put a small gauze pad firmly on but *not in* the tooth socket. It needs to be big enough to project above the level of the remaining teeth.

**3** Tell the casualty to bite hard on the pad for 10–20 minutes. She may find it easier if she puts her elbow on the table and supports her jaw in her cupped hand.

**4** Seek dental or medical aid.

# Bleeding from inside the ear

## Action

**1** Help the casualty into a comfortable position with her head tilted towards the injured side.

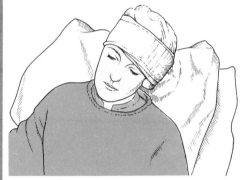

**2** Cover the whole ear with a sterile dressing and secure it lightly with the attached bandage. *Do not put anything inside the ear* in order to stop the flow of blood.

**3** Seek medical aid.

# Bleeding from the nose

## Action

**1** Sit the casualty down and tell him to pinch his nostrils (the soft part of his nose) lean forward and breathe through his mouth; he may need to maintain this pressure for 10–20 minutes. Undo any tight clothing around his neck.

**2** Tell the casualty to spit out any excess fluid in his mouth because swallowing may disturb the clot and make him feel sick. If possible give him a bowl to spit into.

**3** Advise the casualty to avoid touching or blowing his nose for some hours afterwards because he may restart the bleeding.

**4** If the bleeding does not stop, seek medical aid.

## IMPORTANT

If bleeding from the ear or nose follows a blow to a person's head, this could mean that he or she has a fractured skull. If the casualty is conscious, help him or her into a half-sitting position and support the head and shoulders with any pillows or coats available; if he or she is unconscious, treat as on page 67. In either case, transfer the casualty to hospital as soon as possible.

# Bleeding from the scalp

The skin that covers the head, the scalp, has a rich blood supply. When damaged by a fall there may be a gaping wound which bleeds profusely so the injury may appear more serious than it is. However, because a blow to the head can also fracture the skull or cause concussion, all casualties with head injuries must be seen by a doctor (see page 69).

**Action**

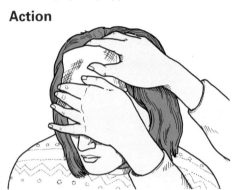

**1** Cover the injury with a clean pad and press the sides of the wound together to control the bleeding.

**2** Place a sterile dressing on the wound and secure it firmly with the bandage (see page 27).

**3** Help the casualty to sit down and support the head and shoulders.

**4** Seek medical aid.

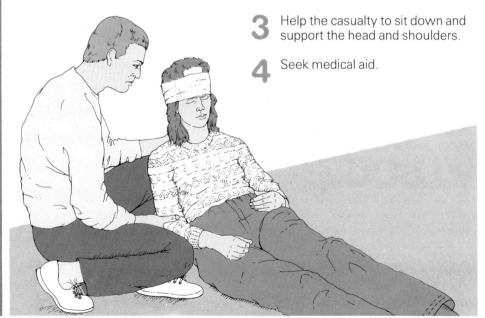

# Bruising

This is bleeding just under the skin or deeper in the tissues following injury which does not break the skin. The area will often become blue/black after quite a short time.

## IMPORTANT

A "black eye" is a bruise normally caused by a blow to the face but as it may also involve damage to the eye or skull, you should always make sure it is seen by a doctor.

**Action**

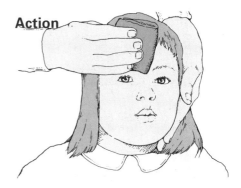

**1** Place a cold compress on the injury to minimise swelling.

**2** Support the injured part in the most comfortable position for the casualty, in a sling if appropriate.

## Cold compresses

These are placed on bruises or sprains to cool the area. This will minimise swelling and therefore reduce the pain.

Leave a compress on an injury for about 30 minutes. If possible leave it uncovered, but if you need to secure it, use an open-weave material such as a gauze bandage.

### Cold water pack
Soak a face cloth, thin towel or similar material in cold water, then wring it out until it stops dripping. Fold it to the required size and place it over the injury. Replace the pack every 10

minutes if possible; otherwise keep it cool by dripping cold water on to it as necessary.

### Ice packs
If you have any ice available you can make a very effective compress by filling a plastic bag half to two-thirds full of ice. Add a little salt — this makes

the ice melt faster — squeeze the air out of the bag and seal it. Wrap the bag in a thin towel and place it over the injury.

# Burns and scalds

If you were shown a section of skin under a microscope, you would see that it is made up of a number of layers. The skin has many functions, one of which is to protect the body from invasion by germs. A burn or scald is an injury which — like any other wound — can break this protective barrier and allow germs to enter the body. This is called "infection".

Burns are caused by extremes of dry heat or cold (cold burns). Fires and hot metal are both sources of dry heat. Scalds, which result in identical injuries, are caused by extremes of moist heat; steam, boiling water and hot fat are all sources of moist heat.

Burns are also caused by strong acids or alkalis (chemical burns); friction, for example, when sliding down a rope (friction burns); exposure to sunlight or any other source of radiation (radiation burns); high-voltage electricity or contact with faulty electrical appliances (electrical burns).

## Consequence of burns or scalds

The main ill-effect which we have already mentioned, is infection. The next is that fluid weeps into and from the tissues. This loss of body fluid depletes the fluid part of the blood (plasma) and if a sufficiently extensive area of skin is burned, even superficially (see below), shock will occur (see page 25). If more than one tenth of the body surface is burned (an area roughly the size of the surface area of the abdomen), you can expect shock to develop. If more than one third of the body surface is burned, the victim's life is in immediate danger and urgent hospital treatment will be required.

## Types of burn

Burns may be divided into two main types — superficial and deep. The depth of the burn which results from exposure to heat depends firstly on the intensity of the heat and secondly the length of time during which the body is exposed to that heat. However, very high temperatures applied for a split second may produce only a superficial burn, whereas less intense heat in contact with the skin over a long period may result in a deep burn.

Superficial burns involve only the surface layers of the skin. Deep burns go right through the full thickness of the skin. Some areas of superficial and others of deep burns may be present in the same casualty. It may be difficult, or even impossible, to tell the difference between superficial and deep burns at first sight. However, the distinction is only of importance to doctors in deciding the final treatment. The first aid treatment for all types remains the same whatever the depth: cool the area as soon as possible, see pages 36 to 37, and seek medical aid.

✚ **Cause**
Look around you; the cause of the injury may still be near the casualty, for example, the iron may be on the floor beside her.

✚ **Danger**
Make sure that neither you nor the casualty is in any further danger; for example, move the iron away and make sure the lead is unplugged.

## Symptoms and signs
These will vary according to the extent of the injury.

+ **Swelling**
This will develop very quickly around any burn.

+ **Shock**
The degree of shock will vary according to the depth and extent of the injury (see page 25).

+ **Redness**
The skin will become red very quickly after a superficial burn.

+ **Charred skin**
If the burn is *deep*, you may notice grey, charred skin.

+ **Blisters**
Small bubbles of fluid known as blisters may develop under the top layer of skin. These may break, leaving a fine layer of skin peeling away and a small red patch weeping fluid. DO NOT BREAK A BLISTER ON PURPOSE.

+ **Pain**
The casualty may complain she is in extreme pain. This is a feature of all burns, although deep burns are sometimes less painful than superficial ones because the nerve ends in the skin will be damaged.

# Treating burns and scalds

Your aim in treating a burn is to reduce the effect of the heat on the skin and as far as possible prevent germs getting into the burnt area. As a general rule, only *very* small superficial burns can be safely treated at home. All other burns should be examined by a doctor or nurse as soon as possible. Casualties suffering from shock need hospital treatment urgently.

### Extensive burns
If a large part of the casualty's body surface is burnt, lay him or her down, protecting any burnt area from contact with the ground, and treat for shock (see page 25). Do not give him or her anything to eat or drink because an anaesthetic may be needed later.

## IMPORTANT

**Never try to remove anything that is sticking to a wound.**

**Never put any fats, lotions or ointments on a burn.**

**Never try to burst a blister caused by a burn.**

**Never put cotton wool directly on a burn.**

**Never use adhesive dressings to cover burns.**

**If there is no water available, use any cold harmless liquid such as milk instead.**

**Immersing infants in cold water for prolonged periods can cause *Hypothermia* (see page 78).**

### Action

**1** Remove the casualty from any danger. Do not let her rush outside if her clothes are on fire.

**2** If the casualty's clothes are on fire, lay her down and douse the flames with water or any non-flammable liquid to hand, or smother the flames by wrapping a blanket, rug or coat around her.

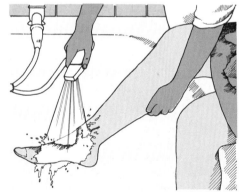

**3** Cool the burnt area immediately. Hold the injured part under cold running water for at least 10 minutes to reduce the pain. If this is not possible, immerse the injured part in a bucket or bath of cold water.

**4** Quickly but carefully remove any rings, watches or tight clothing from the injured area *before* any swelling develops.

**5** Carefully remove or cut away any clothing soaked in boiling fluid or chemical, making sure that you do not burn yourself.

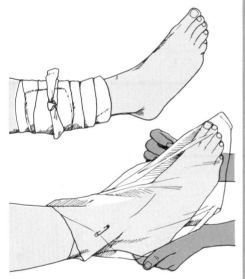

**6** Protect the injury by placing over it a sterile dressing large enough to cover the area completely. If there is no suitable sterile dressing, cover the injured area with a clean handkerchief, towel or sheet. Alternatively, place a clean polythene bag over a hand or foot. Fix the dressing or bag in place with pins or bandages; make sure you allow for swelling.

**7** Watch for any symptoms and signs of shock (see page 27).

**8** Await the arrival of the ambulance.

# Scalded mouth and throat

The mouth, throat and gut are lined with a very thin layer of skin called a mucous membrane. This membrane can be damaged by drinking a very hot fluid, swallowing chemicals which burn or inhaling steam; when damaged the membrane swells very quickly. Severe swelling particularly in the mouth and throat can block the casualty's airway and prevent breathing.

### Symptoms and signs
- If severe, symptoms and signs of shock will develop (see page 25)
- the casualty's mouth and throat are very painful
- difficulty in breathing
- damaged skin around the mouth.

### Action

**1** Reassure the casualty and, if conscious, wash the mouth out with cold water to cool the tissues, then give frequent sips of water to drink.

**2** Quickly remove any jewellery or tight clothing from around the neck and chest.

**3** Get the casualty to hospital as soon as possible.

**4** If the casualty is unconscious, treat as described on page 67.

# Chemical burns

Industrial materials, some household cleaning materials such as caustic soda and bleaches, or workshop materials such as paint stripper can seriously damage the skin or eyes. You must act quickly to wash the chemical off the casualty's skin or out of the eyes but be careful not to injure yourself.

**Action**

*Chemical burns on the skin:*

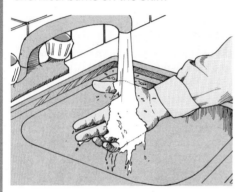

**1** Flood the area by holding the injured part under cold running water for at least 10 minutes.

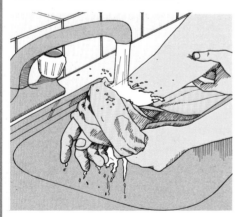

**2** Take any contaminated clothing off the casualty while you are flooding the area.

**3** Continue treatment for burns described on pages 36 to 37.

*Chemical burns of the eye:*

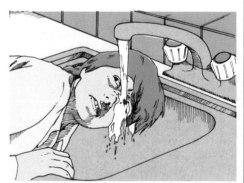

**1** Hold the affected side of the casualty's face under gently running cold water for 10 minutes or longer. If this is not possible, pour the water from a jug. In either case position her head so that contaminated water does not run down her face.

**2** Place a sterile dressing over the eye and lightly secure it.

**3** Take the casualty to hospital as soon as possible.

## IMPORTANT

**Protect your hands from any contact with the chemical.**

**Make sure that the water can drain away freely because it will be contaminated.**

# Sunburn

Over-exposure to the sun's rays without adequate protection can result in widespread superficial burns and sometimes blistering. The skin will become very red and feel very hot. If severe, sunburn can be extremely painful. Remember, sun rays powerful enough to cause sunburn can penetrate cloud or be reflected off bright surfaces such as snow, white walls or concrete.

## Action

**1** Tell the casualty to move into the shade and give him plenty of water to drink.

**2** If the sunburn is mild, special after-sun creams can be applied to relieve the pain.

**3** If you are in any doubt, seek medical advice.

## IMPORTANT

**Prevention is better than cure. Never go out in the sun without protective sunscreen creams and always expose the body gradually. Only small areas of your body should be uncovered for short periods of time.**

# Blisters from rubbing

Blisters develop when skin is damaged by friction or heat; tissue fluid leaks from the damaged area and collects just under the skin. Blisters caused by rubbing, for example, blisters on the heel from a boot, may cause so much discomfort that they need to be broken before the person can continue.

## Action

**1** Wipe the blister with cotton wool soaked in methylated spirit, or wash the area with soap and water.

**2** Sterilise a needle by passing it through a small flame and allow it to cool. Do not wipe the soot away or touch the end of the needle.

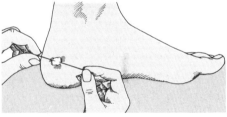

**3** Keeping the needle at the level of the skin, pass it into the blister in two places; ideally you should make one hole on each side.

**4** Place a clean piece of cotton wool on the blister and press out the fluid. *Do not remove the skin.* Cover the blister with a small adhesive dressing.

## IMPORTANT

**Never break a blister caused by contact with heat because of the risk of infection.**

# Triangular bandages

These are normally made from un-
bleached calico. You can make one by
cutting in half diagonally any similar
piece of material approximately 1m
(1yd) square. Triangular bandages are
used to support limbs with broken
bones (see pages 46 to 57) or to secure
light dressings to an injury such as a
burn where you do not need any pressure, see right and opposite.

## Open triangular bandage

When you use an open bandage to
make a sling, for example, fold up a
*narrow* hem along the base to give a
firm edge.

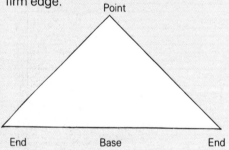

## Broad-fold bandage

Fold the point to the base and then fold
the whole bandage in half again.

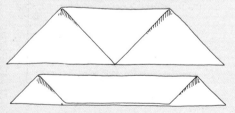

## Narrow-fold bandage

Fold a broad-fold bandage in half again
in the same direction.

## Foot or hand bandage

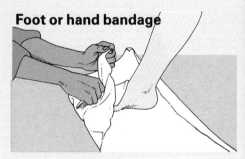

**1** Place the casualty's foot on the
bandage so that the base comes
halfway up her ankle. Bring the point of
the bandage up over her toes to the
front of her ankle.

**2** Carry the ends forward to the front
of her ankle, cross them over, take
them around to the back, cross them
over again and finally tie off in front
below the point using a *reef* knot.

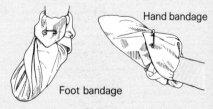

Hand bandage

Foot bandage

**3** Bring the point down over the knot
and secure it to the rest of the
bandage with a safety pin.

**4** Check that the bandage is not too
tight; reapply if necessary.

## Scalp bandage

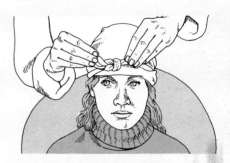

**1** Fold up a hem along the base of a triangular bandage and place the hem on the casualty's forehead so the centre of the base is just above her eyebrows and the point hangs down the back of her head.

**3** Tie the ends in a reef knot on the casualty's forehead as close to the bottom of the hem as possible.

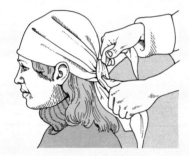

**2** Carry the ends around to the back of her head passing just above her ears. Cross the ends over the point (at the nape of the casualty's neck) and bring them around to the front again.

**4** Steady her head with one hand and gently draw the point down to take up the slack. Turn the point up and secure it on the top of her head with a safety pin.

### Tying a reef knot

Reef knots should always be used to secure bandages because: they will not slip, they lie flat against the casualty and they are easy to undo.

Take one end of the bandage in each hand.

Carry the right end over the left and pass it underneath (A). Then carry what is now the left end over the right end and pass it underneath again (B). Pull the knot tight (C) to secure it.

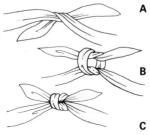

A

B

C

# Broken bones

The body is supported by its own scaffolding of bones called the *skeleton* (see page 44). Normally bones are very strong but they can break or crack if struck, twisted or over-stressed; this injury is known as a *fracture*. A fracture may be caused by *direct force*, in which case the break will be at the point of impact. Alternatively, a break could be caused by *indirect force*, which means that the break occurs at some distance from the point of impact or is the result of a bad twist or strain.

Bones have important blood vessels, nerves and organs lying alongside them so all fractures must be handled carefully. The aim of first aid is to prevent further damage by avoiding unnecessary movement.

Casualties with suspected fractures should as far as possible be treated in the position in which you find them. Steady and support the injured bone by placing one hand above and the other below the site of the injury and await the arrival of the ambulance. If the ambulance is delayed, secure the injured part to a sound part of the body or a rigid support with bandages. This is known as splinting. Specific treatment for the most common fractures is described later in this section. There are, however, general rules of treatment which must be followed for all fractures and these are listed opposite. Always remember, if you are in any doubt about an injury, treat it as a fracture.

## Symptoms and signs

All the general symptoms are indicated in the captions around this photograph. Not all the symptoms and signs listed are present in every case and those that are relevant to particular injuries are listed with the treatments.

**+ Danger**
Make sure the casualty is not in any further danger (for example, from traffic if he is lying on the road surface).

**+ Symptoms and signs of shock**
Shock may develop if a large bone such as the thigh bone is broken because there may be severe internal and/or external bleeding (see page 25).

**+ Pain**
The casualty may complain of extreme pain at the site of the injury.

## IMPORTANT

**Bandages should be firm enough to prevent movement but not too tight. Remember always to allow for swelling, which may develop slowly or very rapidly.**

**+ Hearing a bone break** The casualty may tell you that he heard or felt the bone break as he fell; he may also be able to feel bone ends grating.

**+ Swelling** The area around the injury may appear swollen and bruised; this may not be evident at first.

**+ Deformity** The affected limb or part of the body may appear deformed compared to the other limb or side of the body; for example, one leg may be shorter than the other or the injured limb may be twisted further than is normally possible or it may be bent at an unusual angle.

**+ Movement** The casualty finds it difficult or impossible to move the injured part.

## Action

**1** Steady and support the injured part with both hands by holding it at the joints above and below the fracture site

**2** Always treat the casualty where you find him unless he is in any immediate danger. In that case temporarily immobilise the part as above while other people move him.

**3** Cover any open wound with a sterile dressing. If the bone is sticking out, treat as on page 45.

**4** If removal to hospital is imminent, apply traction to the broken limb as necessary and make the casualty as comfortable as possible while you wait for the transport.

**5** If the ambulance is going to be delayed, secure the injured part to an uninjured part of the body using soft padding and bandages or slings (see pages 46 to 57).

**6** Check the circulation in the hand or foot after bandaging. Is it warm, is it a normal colour? If not, the bandages are too tight.

**7** If possible raise and support an injured limb *after* securing it to minimise discomfort and swelling.

**8** If signs of shock develop; treat as on page 25.

**9** Await the arrival of the ambulance or medical aid.

# The skeleton

The bones that together make up the skeleton protect and surround vital organs and act as levers for muscle to pull against.

The four main parts of the skeleton that protect the vital organs are:

**The skull,** which consists of a number of bones united to form a dome-like vault with a flat base, containing the brain (see page 68).

**The spine,** a column of bones (vertebrae) which extends from the base of the skull all the way down the back and encloses and protects the spinal cord (see page 68). Each bone is separated by a disc or "cushion" of cartilage.

**The ribcage,** consisting of twelve pairs of bones (ribs) which begin at the spine and curve round to meet the breastbone at the front, forming a cage which houses amongst other organs the heart and lungs.

**The pelvis,** which is a "basin" consisting of two hip bones each joined to the bottom section of the spine. The pelvis contains two sockets into which the thigh bones fit, thus forming the hip joints. It surrounds and protects the bladder and bowel. The major blood vessels and nerves that supply the lower limbs pass through the pelvis.

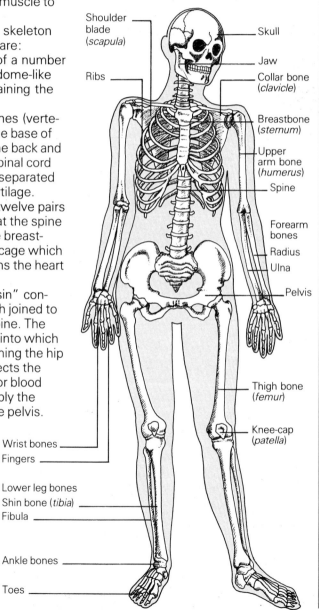

Shoulder blade (*scapula*)

Ribs

Skull

Jaw

Collar bone (*clavicle*)

Breastbone (*sternum*)

Upper arm bone (*humerus*)

Spine

Forearm bones

Radius

Ulna

Pelvis

Thigh bone (*femur*)

Knee-cap (*patella*)

Wrist bones

Fingers

Lower leg bones
Shin bone (*tibia*)
Fibula

Ankle bones

Toes

# Types of fracture

There are many types of fracture but there are two main divisions: closed and open. Closed and open fractures can also be complicated when a broken bone end presses on or damages adjacent nerves, blood vessels or organs.

**Closed fractures** are those where the skin around the break is not damaged. **Open fractures** are fractures where the broken bone end protrudes through the skin or where there is a wound leading down to the fracture.

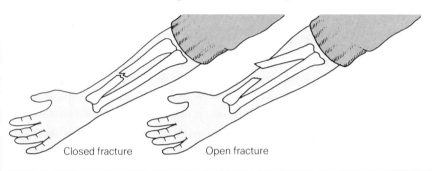

Closed fracture          Open fracture

# Open fractures

This type of injury needs very careful handling because germs can enter the bone and cause serious infection. If there is no bone sticking out of the wound, place a sterile dressing over it.

If the bone is sticking out, treat as described below. Two people will be needed – one person to support the injured limb while another person applies the dressings.

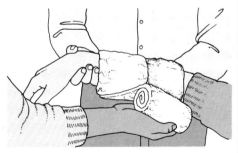

**1** Your helper should support the injured limb by placing one hand above the fracture site and one below.

**2** Drape a piece of gauze over the wound and place cotton wool padding *around* it.

**3** Seek medical aid as soon as possible.

# Lower limb

A fracture of any of the three bones in the leg can be a serious injury. In the lower leg, the shin bone (fibula) is just under the skin and a fracture is often "open"

The thigh bone (femur) is the longest and strongest bone in the body. It has a rich blood supply and a break causes serious internal bleeding. A minor fall can result in a fractured neck of femur, especially in the elderly.

## Immobilisation
Never move a casualty with a fracture unless it has first been immobilised or life is at risk. The joints above and below a break must be kept steady and supported, or immobilised with bandages against the uninjured leg.

## Symptoms and signs
Pain, swelling, loss of movement and shock may be present.
*If the leg is broken below the knee*:
● there may be an open wound if the skin is broken
● the foot may have fallen to one side although the knee is straight.
*If the thigh bone is broken*:
● the injured limb may look shorter than the other one because the thigh muscle may contract
● the foot and knee may have fallen sideways if the neck of femur is broken.

## Action

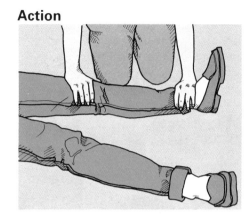

**1** Steady and support the limb holding it at the joints above and below the fracture. Get a bystander to do this if possible.

**2** Treat any wounds, if present.

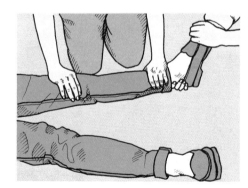

**3** Holding the ankle and foot, apply gentle traction, carefully pulling in the long axis of the limb to bring it into its normal line.

**4** *If the ambulance is imminent*, maintain the injured limb in this position. Treat the casualty for *shock* (see page 25).

# Thigh bone

**1** Steps 1 and 2 for lower limb.

**2** Apply and maintain gentle traction by holding the casualty's knee. Meanwhile, the assistant should gently straighten the lower leg. Bring the injured leg into a straight line by pulling in the long axis of the limb from the ankle.

**3** Step 4 for lower limb.

*If the ambulance is delayed*, support the injured leg at the ankle and, using the natural hollows, gently place broad-fold bandages under the casualty's legs at the knees and above and below the fracture, and a narrow-fold bandage under the ankles. Place padding between the legs for step 6, left.

**4** Avoiding jerky movements, tie the knots on the uninjured side. Tie a figure-of-eight bandage around the ankles and feet, then the bandage at the knees, above the fracture and finally the one below the fracture.

**5** *If the ambulance is delayed*, continue supporting the limb and, using the natural hollows, gently place *broad-fold bandages* (see page 40) under the casualty's legs at the knees, above and below the fracture and a *narrow-fold bandage* (see page 40) under the ankles.

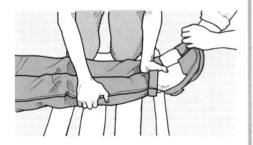

**6** Gently bring the sound limb alongside the injured one. Place adequate soft padding between the legs to cushion the ankles and knees and further padding to fill the natural hollow so that the bandages do not displace the bones.

**7** Tie the knots on the uninjured side, starting with the figure-of-eight bandage at the ankles, then the knee bandage, then above and below the fracture. *If the fracture is near the ankle, modify the ankle bandage so that it is not over the fracture.*

## IMPORTANT

**When traction is being applied, if any resistance is felt, *stop immediately*. Never leave a casualty's lower limb unsupported.**

# Pelvis

A fractured pelvis must be handled with great care because there may be internal injuries.

### Symptoms and signs
If the pelvis is fractured, most of the general symptoms and signs listed on page 42 will be evident.
*The casualty may tell you that she*:
● is unable to move the lower part of

her body without extreme pain and that the area around her pelvis is very tender and uncomfortable.
● is unable to stand.
*If the fracture is complicated, you may notice that*:
● any urine passed by the casualty is blood-stained
● there are signs of severe internal bleeding (see *Shock* page 25).

### Action

**1** Help the casualty to lie on her back with her legs straight or with knees slightly bent with a cushion or rolled coat under them, whichever she finds the most comfortable.

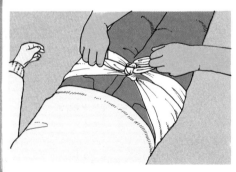

**2** Pass two *broad-fold bandages* (see page 40) around her hips and pelvis, one slightly above the first and overlapping it by half. (Slide one end of the bandage through the hollow under her back and ease it into position.) Tie the knots in the centre of the body.

**3** Place some soft padding between the casualty's knees and ankles.

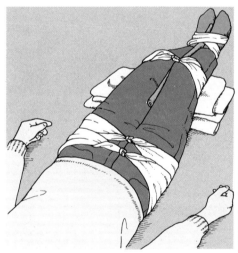

**4** Tie her feet and ankles together with a *narrow-fold bandage* (see page 40) tied in a figure of eight and place a *broad-fold bandage* around both her knees.

**5** Treat the casualty as described on page 25 to prevent shock.

**6** Await the arrival of the ambulance or medical aid.

# Spine

A fractured spine can be a very serious injury because the spinal cord which runs down the spine contains the nerves that control many of the functions of the body (see page 68). Damage to the spinal cord can result in loss of power in the parts of the body below the injured area.

A sudden bending or twisting of the back or neck may result in a sprain of the ligaments supporting the spine or injury to the discs between the bones of the spine. A more violent bending or twisting or a direct blow may damage one or more of the bones. If the bones or pieces of bone are then displaced, the spinal cord may be damaged. A mild injury can be made considerably worse by incorrect handling.

You should suspect a spine injury if you find someone who has fallen awkwardly and landed on his or her back, for example, falling down the stairs or off a ladder.

## Symptoms and signs

*The casualty may tell you that she:*
● is tender around the affected part of her back
● can feel shooting pains or "electric shocks" in her limbs and/or around her trunk
● is unable to feel or move her legs if the injury is in the lower back or to move any limb at all if the injury is at neck level.

## IMPORTANT

**Do not move the casualty unless his or her life is in danger. Moving a casualty with a fractured spine is a very skilled procedure which should be carried out only by at least four to six skilled first aiders under qualified supervision.**

## Action

**1** Advise the casualty not to move.

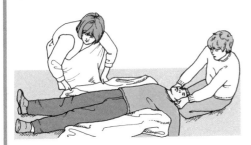

**2** Make her as comfortable as possible in the position in which you find her. Steady her head by hand and place rolled coats and/or pillows along either side of her body and legs and cover her with a blanket.

**3** If the ambulance is delayed, reassure the casualty and remind her not to move. Loosen tight clothing and ensure the head and shoulders are steadied and well-supported.

**4** Await the arrival of the ambulance.

# Knee

The knee-cap can be broken by a direct blow or split by violent muscular pull from the thigh muscles which are attached to it. All knee injuries are very painful and it may be difficult to tell whether a person has a broken knee-cap or has damaged a cartilage or ligament (see page 60). If in doubt treat as described below.

## Symptoms and signs

General symptoms and signs of fracture will be present.
*The casualty may tell you that*:
● her knee is extremely painful
● she is unable to lift her leg or foot off the ground.
*You may notice that*:
● the affected knee is bent and any attempt to straighten it increases the pain considerably
● the joint swells up very quickly and feels tense.

## Action

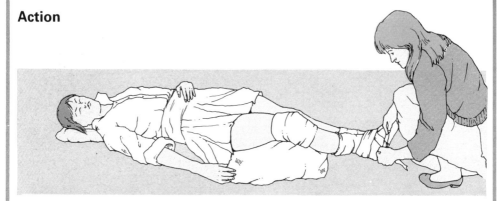

**1** Help the casualty to lie down on her back and steady her leg in the position she finds the most comfortable. Place a small pillow in the hollow under her knee and rolled coats and/or pillows around her leg.

## IMPORTANT

**Do not force the leg straight.**

**2** Bandaging is not essential but the casualty may find it more comfortable. Surround the knee with cotton wool padding – a roll of cotton wool is ideal – then bandage carefully allowing for swelling.

**3** For extra support, tie a *narrow-fold bandage* (see page 40) in a figure of eight around the casualty's feet and ankles; tie the knot against the side of the casualty's foot.

**4** Await the arrival of the ambulance.

# Jaw

The jaw-bone can be fractured by a blow to the face. This injury may be complicated by mouth wounds which can cause breathing difficulties.

## Symptoms and signs
*You may notice*:
- that the casualty finds it difficult to speak, chew or swallow without increased pain and she may be dribbling
- blood-stained saliva if there is a mouth wound
- displaced teeth in the mouth
- swelling and/or unevenness along one side of the jaw.

## Action

**1** Carefully remove any *loose* objects such as dentures or displaced teeth from her mouth and help her to lean forward so that any fluid can drain freely. Keep these teeth and give them to the doctor or ambulance driver.

**2** Place a soft pad over the site of injury and hold it in place with the palm of your hand; the casualty may be able to do this herself.

**3** If necessary, secure the pad by tying a *narrow-fold bandage* (see page 40) around her head so that the knot is on the top of her head.

## IMPORTANT

**If the casualty is seriously injured or unconscious but breathing normally, place her in the *recovery position* (see page 14) with the injured side down and a soft pad under her head to keep the weight off her jaw.**

**4** If the casualty appears likely to be sick, quickly remove the bandage and support her jaw.

**5** Await the arrival of the ambulance or medical aid.

# Ribs

Broken ribs are splinted naturally because they are attached to the rest of the ribcage. Treatment of a broken rib therefore involves immobilising only the upper limb on the affected side of the body to help relieve pain.

## Symptoms and signs

The general symptoms and signs of fracture, such as pain increased by movement and some swelling, will be present. In addition, *the casualty may tell you he*:

● feels a very sharp pain in his side, worsened by taking deep breaths or by coughing

● is particularly tender around the affected ribs

● can hear a crackling sound.

## Action

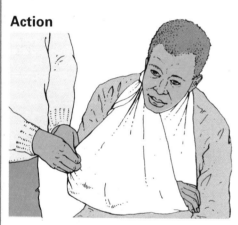

**1** Help the casualty to sit down and support the arm on his injured side in an *arm sling* (see page 56).

**2** Take him to hospital.

## IMPORTANT

**Chest injuries involving damage to several ribs or the lungs are more serious and require urgent medical attention because there may be breathing difficulties.**

*If the fracture is complicated*:

**1** Help the casualty into a half-sitting position so that he is leaning towards his injured side.

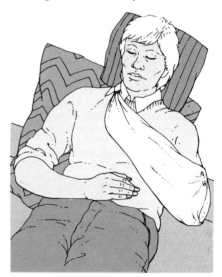

**2** Support the arm on the injured side with an *elevation sling* (see page 57).

**3** Await the arrival of the ambulance.

# Collar bone

The most common cause of a broken collar bone is a fall on to an outstretched hand where the force is transmitted along the forearm and upper arm to the collar bone.

## Symptoms and signs

Characteristically a casualty with a broken collar bone will be supporting her arm on the injured side and inclining her head towards the injury to relieve the pain:

● she will be reluctant to move her arm on the injured side
● swelling or deformity may be visible at the site of injury.

**Action**

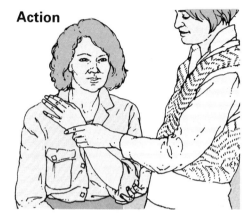

**1** Help the casualty position her arm on the injured side so that her fingertips are almost resting on the opposite shoulder.

**2** Support the arm in an *elevation sling* (see page 57) and place soft padding between upper arm and chest.

**3** Secure the limb to the casualty's chest by applying a *broad-fold bandage* (see page 40) over the sling and right around her body.

**4** Take the casualty to hospital.

# Upper limb

A break can occur anywhere along the length of the upper arm or forearm bones or in the hand and sometimes involves the elbow or wrist joints.

## Symptoms and signs

These will be the same as for all fractures: pain, tenderness, inability to use the injured arm, deformity, swelling and possible bruising. In particular, the casualty will probably be supporting the hand, forearm and elbow of the injured arm with the other arm.

### Action

**1** If possible gently bend the casualty's arm at the elbow so that her forearm is across her chest and place soft padding between the fracture site and her body.

**3** For additional support, secure the casualty's arm to her trunk by applying a *broad-fold bandage* (see page 40) right around her arm and trunk. Avoid the fracture site.

**4** Take the casualty to hospital.

**2** Support her arm with an *arm sling* (see page 56).

## IMPORTANT

**Never bend the arm forcibly.**

**Check the circulation after bandaging by looking at the fingers; are they warm, are the nails the right colour (see step 6, page 43)? Relax the sling if necessary.**

## If the arm cannot be bent

**1** Help the casualty to lie down with his arm by his side, or wherever it is most comfortable for him.

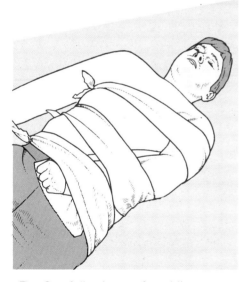

**2** Carefully place soft padding between the injured limb and the casualty's body and apply three *broad-fold bandages* around the arm and the body, avoiding the fracture site.

**3** Await the arrival of the ambulance.

## Broken hand or fingers

Fractures of the hand or fingers are commonly caused by crushing and the fracture is often open with severe bleeding.

### Action

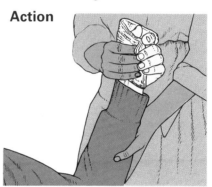

**1** Raise the injured hand to control bleeding and apply a dressing (see page 23).

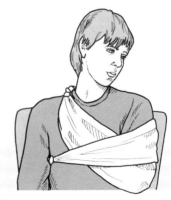

**2** Place the casualty's hand in soft padding and in an *elevation sling* (see page 57) and a *broadfold bandage* (see page 40).

**3** Take the casualty to hospital.

# Slings

There are two types of sling: arm and elevation slings. *Arm slings* are commonly used to support injuries to the upper limb or to immobilise an upper limb in the case of chest injury, but they are effective only if the casualty can sit or stand. *Elevation slings* are used to support a hand in a well-raised position to control bleeding or to immobilise the upper limb if there is a broken collar bone or there are rib injuries.
Always use a triangular bandage (see page 40) or similar-sized piece of material if available. If there is nothing readily available, improvise as described opposite.

**IMPORTANT**

**Always keep an arm supported until the sling is secure.**

### Arm sling

**1** With the casualty sitting down, ask her to support her forearm on the injured side so that her wrist is slightly higher than her elbow; be prepared to help.

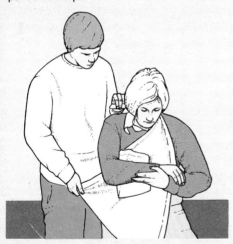

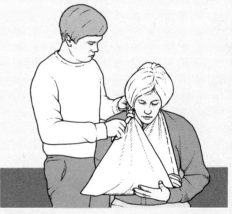

**3** Bring the lower end of the bandage up over the forearm so the edge lies at the base of the little finger. Tie off with a reef knot (see page 41) in the hollow above the collar bone on the injured side.

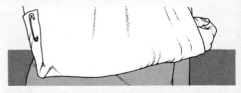

**2** Fold a small hem along the base of a triangular bandage. Slide one end of the bandage through the hollow between the elbow and chest. Pull it up so that the upper end reaches over the shoulder, around the back of the neck to the front, leaving the point beyond the elbow.

**4** Tuck the excess bandage behind the elbow, bring the point around to the front and pin it to the bandage.

## Elevation sling

**1** Support the casualty's arm on the injured side and place it across his chest so that his fingers almost rest on the opposite shoulder.

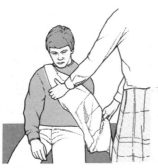

**2** Lay an open bandage over the casualty's arm so that one end is over his shoulder and the point reaches well beyond his elbow.

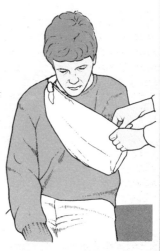

**3** Tuck the base of the bandage under the casualty's forearm and elbow and take the lower end around his back and up towards the other shoulder.

**4** Tie both ends together in the hollow above the collar bone using a *reef knot* (see page 41).

**5** Tuck the point in between the casualty's forearm and the front of the bandage, making a neat fold. Turn this fold up over his arm and pin it to the upper part of the bandage.

## Emergency slings

- Support the arm with a belt, braces, tie or tights tied around the neck. Never use this method if the forearm is broken.

- If the casualty is wearing a coat or waistcoat, place her injured arm inside the fastening. If possible attach the cuff to the lapel with a safety pin.

- If the casualty is wearing a button-up jacket, you can turn the bottom of the jacket up over the injured arm and pin it to the jacket.

# Joint and muscle injuries

Sprains and dislocations, that is injuries to the joints between the bones, or strains, injuries to the muscles that move the bones, are fairly common and can be extremely painful. In some instances, particularly dislocated joints, it can be difficult to distinguish between this type of injury and a broken bone. If you are in any doubt, treat it as a break and seek medical aid.

## Sprained joint

This occurs when the ligaments that hold the bones together at the joints (see page 60) are over-stretched or torn. This is sometimes very painful and may be mistaken for a broken bone.

**Symptoms and signs**
In many cases these are similar to those that are apparent if a bone is actually broken.

**+ Pain**
The casualty will tell you that the area around the affected joint is extremely painful and tender and pain is increased by movement.

**+ Bruising**
Discoloration may develop around the injured area; this will be gradual.

**+ Swelling**
The joint will swell up; this may be gradual or it can be immediate.

+ **Cause**
The casualty may be able to tell you what happened, for example, that he twisted his foot on the edge of the pavement and fell.

+ **Movement**
The casualty may not be able to move the joint and if the injury is at the knee or ankle may not be able to stand on the affected limb.

## Action

This is abbreviated as **RICE**. **R:** *Rest*, **I:** *Ice*, **C:** *Compression*, **E:** *Elevation*.

**1** *Rest* and raise the injured part in the most comfortable position.

**2** Apply an *I*ce pack or cold pack (see page 33) to reduce blood flow and minimise swelling.

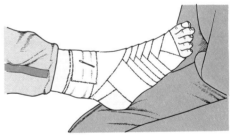

**3** *Compress* the injury with a thick layer of cotton wool and a firm bandage to counteract swelling.

**4** *Elevate* the injured limb. If the injury is to the wrist, elbow or shoulder, support with an *arm sling* (see pages 56 to 57).

**5** Seek medical aid for X-ray diagnosis.

# Joints

Formed where two or more bones meet, joints are held together by tough bands of fibre called LIGAMENTS. The adjoining bone ends are covered by a layer of gristle called CARTILAGE so that they move freely against each other. Joints are surrounded by a membrane which produces a lubricating fluid.

Joints are classified by the movement produced. The most important are the hinge joints, such as the knee and elbow joints, which allow to-and-fro movement in one plane only; and the ball-and-socket joints, such as the hip and shoulder joints, which permit pivoting and rotation of the limb.

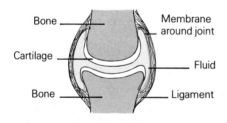

Bone ———————— Membrane around joint

Cartilage ————

———— Fluid

Bone ———————— Ligament

# Muscles

Bones are moved at the joints by muscles. Each muscle consists of a fleshy part known as the "belly", which is attached directly to a bone. At the other end the muscle tapers, ending in a narrow, fibrous TENDON, which is attached to another bone. Movement occurs when a muscle contracts and pulls one bone towards another.

# Dislocated joint

A dislocation is the displacement of bones at a joint. It is normally caused by a particularly violent or sudden twisting strain on the joint, which tears the ligaments supporting it.

## IMPORTANT

**Never try to manipulate a dislocated joint.**

**Move the affected limb as little as possible.**

# Knee injuries

Common knee injuries include sprain (see page 58), displaced cartilage and fractured knee-cap (see page 50).

Two pads of cartilage lie between the upper surface of the shin bone and the base of the thigh bone. If the knee is wrenched suddenly while the foot remains on the ground, one or both of these pads can be torn and/or displaced. This is a common sporting injury and can be extremely painful. In some cases it is very difficult to tell the difference between this and a broken knee-cap. If in doubt, treat as a fracture (see page 50).

## Symptoms and signs

*The casualty may tell you she*:
● feels a sickening pain around the affected joint
● is unable to move the affected joint.
*You may notice*:
● swelling around the affected joint
● severe deformity at the site of injury, particularly when compared with the other side of the body.

## Action

**1** Help the casualty into the position she finds most comfortable. Support the injured limb with pillows, rolled blankets and/or an *arm sling* (see page 56) as applicable.

**2** Await the arrival of an ambulance or medical aid.

## Symptoms and signs

*The casualty may tell you he*:
● feels severe, even sickening, pain around the affected knee
● is unable to move the affected knee; the knee will probably be bent and any attempt to straighten it will make the pain even worse
● heard a snap or "clunk" in his knee as he fell.
*You may notice*:
● rapid and severe swelling in and around the knee joint.

## Action

**1** Immobilise the casualty's leg by surrounding it with pillows and/or rolled blankets.

**2** Await the arrival of an ambulance or medical aid.

**3** Bandaging is not essential although the casualty may find it more comfortable. Surround the knee with cotton wool – a roll of cotton wool is ideal for this – and bandage carefully allowing for swelling.

**4** Support the casualty's injured leg with both hands while he is placed on the stretcher.

# Strained muscle

Muscles and their tendons can be strained or torn by any sudden violent contraction or awkward movement. Also referred to as a "pulled muscle", this is a common sports injury. More rarely, a muscle can be torn in half.

## Symptoms and signs

*The casualty may tell you:*
- the injured part hurts when he tries to repeat the movement that caused injury
- the affected part feels stiff; this may develop very gradually if the casualty has been sitting or lying still.

*You may notice:*
- swelling and discoloration around the site of injury
- a dent in the affected muscle if it has been torn in half.

# Cramp

This is sudden pain in a limb caused by a tightening, or contraction, of a muscle or group of muscles. It can normally be relieved by stretching the affected muscles again.

A person who has been sweating heavily may develop cramp. To relieve this, give him or her a tumbler of water containing a quarter of a teaspoonful of salt (see *Heat exhaustion*, page 80).

## Action

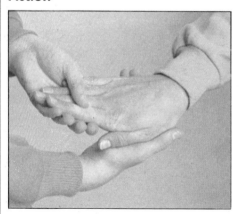

**Cramp in the hand** Straighten the bent fingers by stretching them backwards.

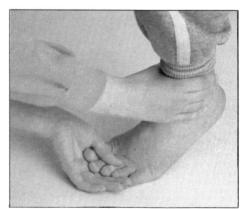

**Cramp in the foot** Straighten the casualty's bent toes by pushing them upwards and help her to stand on the ball of her foot.

## Action

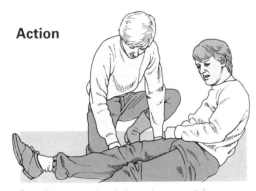

**1** Support the injured part with your hands and help the casualty to *R*est the area.

**2** Apply an *I*ce pack or cold pack (see page 33) to reduce blood flow and minimise swelling.

**3** *C*ompress the injured area with a thick layer of cotton wool and a crepe bandage (see page 64).

**4** *E*levate and support the injured area as appropriate.

**5** If the injury is severe, take the casualty to hospital; otherwise advise him to see a doctor.

### Cramp in the thigh
Straighten the casualty's knee: pull her lower limb up and forwards, and gently but firmly press the knee down.

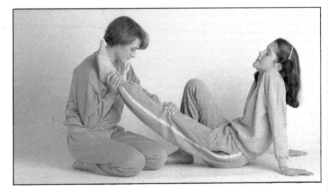

### Cramp in the calf
Straighten the casualty's knee and pull her foot up towards the shin as far as it will go.

# Roller bandages

The most effective bandage for supporting a muscle or joint injury is a roller bandage. This can also be used to secure a dressing and apply pressure to control bleeding. Standard bandages are made of gauze, cotton or linen and they are normally sold in 5m (5yd) lengths. They are available in a variety of widths to fit the different parts of the body to be bandaged. *Crepe* bandages and *conforming* bandages are very useful because they are made of a stretchy material which moulds to the shape of the body, keeping the pressure even.

## RULES FOR APPLYING BANDAGES

- Always stand in front of the casualty
- support the limb or part of the body in the position in which it is to remain
- make sure that the bandage is tightly rolled before you begin
- hold the bandage with the rolled part (head) uppermost
- begin below the injury and work up the limb, from the inner side outward
- make sure the bandage is not too tight (see step 6, page 43).

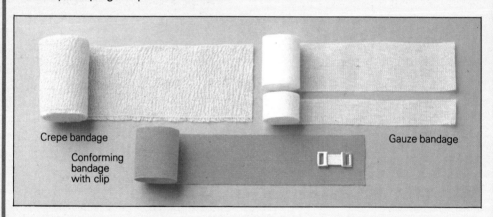

Crepe bandage

Conforming bandage with clip

Gauze bandage

## Ankle bandage

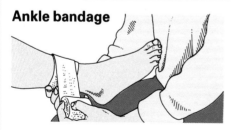

**1** Raise and support the casualty's foot. Make one straight turn around her ankle in order to secure the bandage.

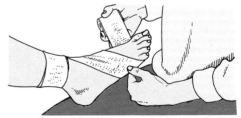

**2** Take the bandage diagonally across the top of her foot towards the base of her little toe. Bring it down around the ball of her foot, and up at the base of her big toe.

## Spiral bandage

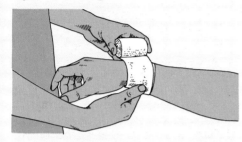

**1** Place the tail of the bandage on the limb and make a firm straight turn to secure the bandage.

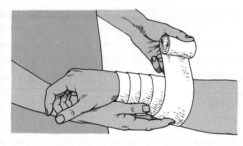

**2** Working up the limb, make a series of spiral turns, allowing each successive turn to cover two thirds of the previous one.

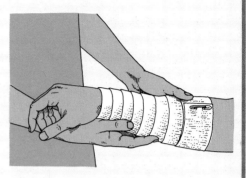

**3** Finish off with a straight turn and secure the end with a safety pin, adhesive tape or a bandage clip.

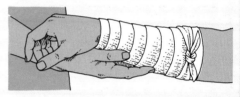

**4** If pins, tape or clips are not available, leave about 15cm (6in) or more of the bandage free (enough to wind around the limb) and cut it down the middle. Tie a knot at the bottom of the split and tie the ends around the limb in a reef knot (see page 41).

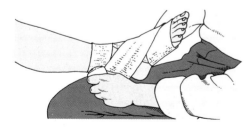

**3** Make two straight turns around the ball of the casualty's foot. Carry the bandage across the top of her foot again.

**4** Continue making figure of eight turns around the foot and ankle until her foot is covered. Finish off by making a final straight turn around her ankle and secure as in 3 or 4 above.

# Unconsciousness

The movement and functions of the body are controlled by the nervous system — the brain, spinal cord and nerves (see page 68). Unconsciousness is a state in which the casualty becomes insensible because of an interruption in the normal function of the brain. It differs from sleep in that you cannot wake the person by shouting at him or her or by using some painful stimulus such as a pinch. Moreover, the normal reflexes such as coughing, which enable you to breathe without choking while asleep, may not work properly or may not work at all.

## Causes of unconsciousness

This condition may develop gradually or suddenly and it can be the result of an injury or an illness. Common causes of unconsciousness include:

● head injury
● conditions that prevent blood containing oxygen getting to the brain, such as, heart failure, severe bleeding, blockage in the arteries which supply blood to the brain (stroke), or fainting.
● something that prevents oxygen entering the lungs, for example, chest injuries, electrical injury, blocked airway (see page 12), lack of oxygen in the air
● poisoning (see page 74)
● some illnesses or conditions such as epilepsy (see page 70), hysteria (see page 71), diabetes, extreme cold or heat exhaustion (see pages 78 to 81).

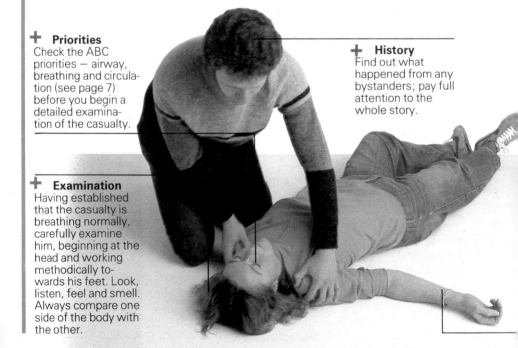

**+ Priorities**
Check the ABC priorities — airway, breathing and circulation (see page 7) before you begin a detailed examination of the casualty.

**+ History**
Find out what happened from any bystanders; pay full attention to the whole story.

**+ Examination**
Having established that the casualty is breathing normally, carefully examine him, beginning at the head and working methodically towards his feet. Look, listen, feel and smell. Always compare one side of the body with the other.

## Levels of consciousness

The casualty may pass through various levels of confusion and stupor (behaving rather like a drunk person) before becoming completely unconscious (coma) and again as he or she recovers consciousness. It is very important that you stay with the casualty all the time and watch him or her constantly, noting *any* changes in the state of awareness because it may help the doctor in deciding what treatment to give later.

## IMPORTANT

**Your most important task as first aider is to maintain an open and clear airway until an ambulance or medical aid arrives.**

**Never leave an unconscious person alone.**

**Anyone who has been unconscious even for a short time or who has had a head injury *must* be seen by a doctor.**

**Do not give the casualty *anything* to eat or drink.**

✚ **External clues** While you examine the casualty, look out for any medical warning signs such as Medic-alert bracelets or information cards worn or carried by those who are liable to a condition that may cause unconsciousness, for example, epilepsy.

Medic-alert bracelet

## Action

**1** Ask the casualty what happened. Gently shake him by the shoulders or pinch his ear lobes.

**2** *Open the airway* (see page 13) if no response. Tilt the head back and lift the lower jaw well forward.

**3** *Check breathing* (see page 13). Look, listen and feel for any signs of breathing. If noisy, *clear the airway* (see page 13). If the casualty is still not breathing, begin *mouth-to-mouth ventilation* (see page 14) immediately.

**4** *Check circulation* (see page 16) by feeling for the carotid artery pulse. If no pulse, begin *external chest compression* (see page 16).

**5** Continue with resuscitation until breathing is spontaneous.

**6** Once the casualty is breathing, loosen tight clothing and examine quickly for signs of serious injury. Control any severe bleeding and support suspected fractures.

**7** If the casualty is breathing regularly, place him in the *recovery position* (see page 18).

**8** If a spinal injury is suspected, do not turn the casualty unless poor breathing makes this essential.

**9** While waiting for the ambulance, keep the airway open, check breathing and pulse and level of consciousness and note any changes.

# Nervous system

This consists of the brain, the spinal cord and the nerves and it operates rather like a large telephone exchange.

The BRAIN is the central exchange which controls the rest of the system. It is a delicate structure made up of a mass of nerve tissue and is encased by the skull. The SPINAL CORD is a rope-like structure of nerves which extends from the base of the brain, down the neck and all the way down the back like a main telephone cable carrying wires to and from the different parts of a town. The spinal cord is surrounded and protected by the bones of the spinal column. Individual NERVES emerge from the spinal cord; they extend from the spinal column to every part of the body, carrying messages to and from every part of the body, like the wires that go to individual telephones.

The illustration, right, shows you very simply and diagrammatically how each part of the nervous system relates to another and to the rest of the body. Damage *anywhere* in the system can result in temporary or permanent loss of power or feeling in that part of the body served by the affected nerves.

**Position of brain**
The brain sits on the base of the skull which is level with your eyes, ears and nose.

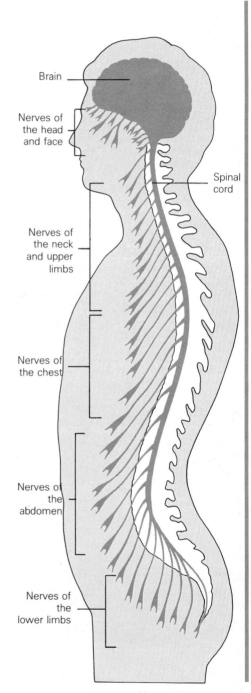

Brain

Nerves of the head and face

Spinal cord

Nerves of the neck and upper limbs

Nerves of the chest

Nerves of the abdomen

Nerves of the lower limbs

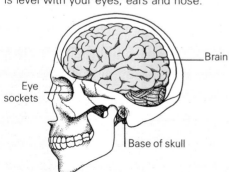

Brain

Eye sockets

Base of skull

# Head injuries

Any blow to the head heavy enough to cause a bruise or a scalp wound could also fracture the skull. Moreover, whether or not the skull is fractured, the blow could result in a condition of unconsciousness known as *concussion*. This is caused by a temporary disturbance or shake up of the brain within the skull — like a jelly wobbling in a mould. Concussion can also result from indirect force such as falling from a height and landing heavily on your feet or by a direct blow on the jaw. It is normally accompanied by a short loss of consciousness although sometimes this is so short that neither you nor the casualty will be aware of it.

It is very important that a person with a head injury is seen by a doctor as soon as possible because there may be delayed effects, such as swelling of the brain, or bleeding into the brain or between the brain and the skull, which cause unconsciousness to deepen.

## Symptoms and signs
*Concussion*:
- a period of unconsciousness
- the casualty may be dazed and confused as she regains consciousness
- the casualty may vomit
- the casualty may not remember the incident or anything that happened immediately before.

*If there is a skull fracture there may be*:
- blood or blood-stained fluid coming from inside the ear or nose
- discoloration (bruising) around the eyelids or on the white part of the eye
- bleeding from the scalp
- possible open fracture; this is a particularly dangerous sign.

*if complications develop*:
- the pupils of the eyes (the black part)

may be abnormal or of different sizes
- the pulse rate may become unusually slow.

## Action

**1** If the casualty does not appear to be seriously injured, advise her to see a doctor as soon as possible; there could be a delayed reaction.

**2** If the casualty was unconscious even for a short time, arrange for her to be taken to hospital.

**3** If you are in any doubt about the casualty's condition or if she is unconscious, follow the steps described on page 67 for treating an unconscious casualty. Remember you must keep the airway open if necessary by placing the casualty in the *recovery position* (see page 18).

**4** Treat any wounds or fractures.

---

## IMPORTANT

**If any complications develop, *urgent* transfer to hospital by ambulance is required.**

# Epilepsy

This is a tendency to fits or seizures which are caused by a brief disturbance in the electrical activity of the brain — the effect is rather like an electrical storm in the brain.

There are two main types of fit: major fits (see below) or minor fits. Do not be frightened when you see a person having a major fit, act as described right. Minor fits can pass unnoticed — the person may just appear to be day-dreaming. Most people who are liable to epileptic fits carry orange warning cards or wear a Medic-alert bracelet.

## Symptoms and signs

Major fits normally follow a pattern of rigidity and loss of consciousness followed by convulsive moments (jerking):
- sudden collapse; casualty some-times lets out a strange cry
- the muscles stiffen, then relax, then begin jerking movements — these may be quite violent

- froth or bubbles may appear around the casualty's mouth — these will be blood-stained if the inside of the mouth or the tongue is bitten
- after the fit is over, usually five minutes at the most, the casualty will regain consciousness but may be dazed and confused. This may last for up to an hour and she may want to rest.

## Action

**1** Keep calm and prevent anyone rushing to the casualty. There is very little you can do; *let the fit run its course without interference.*

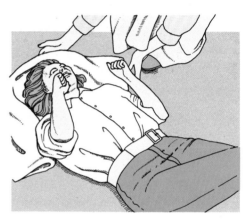

**2** Clear a space around the casualty so that she does not hurt herself, or move her out of the way of traffic. If possible place some soft padding under or around her head.

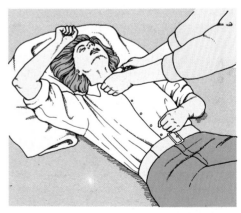

**3** Loosen any tight clothing around her neck — do this very carefully as it is easy to frighten a semi-conscious person.

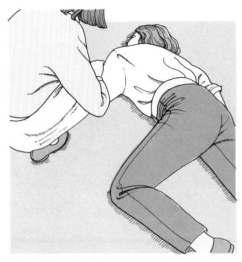

# Hysteria

This is a loss of control of behaviour or emotion. It is usually the result of an over-reaction to anxiety or worries, but there may be no obvious cause. The person is not in any danger although he or she would probably hope that the on-looker might believe otherwise. Even if the person tries to hold his or her breath, eventually the victim will have to breathe again.

## Symptoms and signs
● the casualty behaves strangely; he may be waving arms and legs about
● the casualty may start shouting and screaming or go into a trance-like state – staring blankly ahead. It may be difficult to tell the difference between the trance and other forms of un-consciousness.

**4** When the jerking stops, turn the casualty into the *recovery position* (see page 18).

**5** When the attack is over, stay with the casualty until you are sure she has competely recovered and is able to get home.

## IMPORTANT

**Never try to hold someone down or stop the convulsions.**

**Never put anything in the casu-alty's mouth.**

**Never try to give a person any-thing to eat or drink during a fit.**

**Do not call an ambulance unless one fit follows another without the person regaining conscious-ness in between.**

## Action

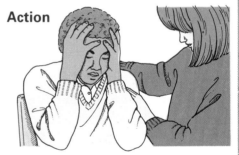

**1** Reassure the casualty but be firm and understanding. Ask any on-lookers to move away – an hysteric will play up to an audience.

**2** When he has calmed down, advise the person to see a doctor.

**3** If you are in any doubt about the casualty's condition, or if he is un-conscious, place him in the *recovery position* (see page 18) and seek medical aid.

# Convulsions in young children

These occur mainly in children between the ages of one and four and are commonly caused by a very high temperature (fever), serious tummy upset, fright or temper. Although they look alarming they are not dangerous.

## Symptoms and signs
● the child may be flushed and sweating with a very hot forehead
● the child may stiffen and his back may be arched
● eyes may be rolled upwards
● the face may appear blue if the child is holding his breath.

**Action**

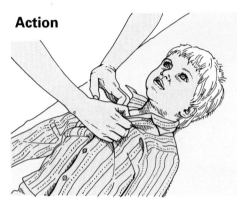

**1** Loosen any tight clothing around the child's neck and chest.

**2** Clear a space around him if convulsions are severe and wipe any froth from around his mouth.

# Fainting

This is a very short loss of consciousness which occurs when the flow of blood to the brain is temporarily reduced. This is sometimes known as "nervous shock" because it can be brought on by pain or emotion. It can also occur if someone has to stand still for a long time in a warm atmosphere; moving the feet and/or changing position can help prevent this. Recovery is normally rapid and complete when the casualty lies down with his or her legs raised above chest height.

## Symptoms and signs
● the casualty will feel weak, faint and giddy and may feel sick
● skin will be very pale
● pulse will be *slow*.

**Action**

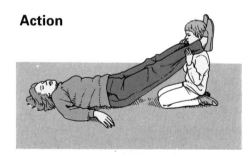

**1** If possible help the casualty to lie down and raise her feet above the level of her heart (chest). If there is no room to lie down, help her to lean forward with her head down between her knees.

**2** Loosen any tight clothing around her neck, chest and waist.

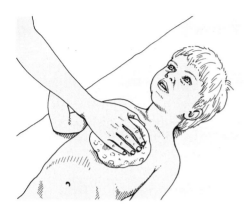

**3** Cool the child by removing his bedclothes and sponging him down with tepid water; work from the head down. Do not let him get too cold.

**4** When the convulsions stop, place the child in the *recovery position* (see page 18) and cover him with light bedclothes. Reassure him.

**5** Seek medical aid.

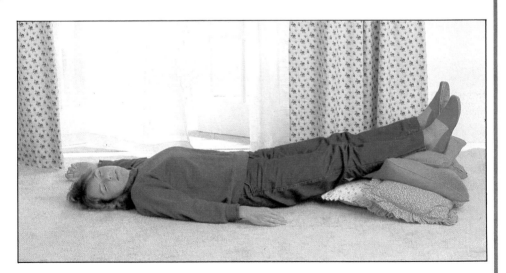

**3** Make sure the casualty has enough air. Open the window and/or ask people not to crowd her; fan her face if necessary.

**4** If in any doubt about her condition, seek medical aid.

# Poisoning

Poisons are substances that result in temporary or permanent damage to the body if taken in sufficient quantities. They may enter the body in several different ways:

- by being swallowed
- by being breathed in (inhaling)
- by being injected under the skin, for example, by hypodermic syringe, animal or insect bites or stings
- by absorption through the skin when using agricultural or garden weedkillers or insecticides, for example.

## Symptoms and signs

These will vary according to the poison and how it was taken. We have listed the main points to look for around this photograph. Try to find out what was taken and how much by asking both the casualty and bystanders if there are any. Remember to ask a conscious casualty what happened quickly because he or she may lose consciousness.

**+ Vomiting**
If the poison has been swallowed, the person may vomit or, at a later stage, be suffering from diarrhoea.

**+ Cause**
There may be a container near the casualty which is known to have or have had a poisonous substance in it.

**+ Fits**
The casualty may be having a fit.

# IMPORTANT

**Keep all poisons locked away.**

**Take care not to get any of the poison on yourself.**

**If the casualty has taken a corrosive poison, never try to force him or her to vomit; a substance that burns going down the gullet will burn again coming up.**

**Do not leave the casualty alone.**

✚ **Burns**
If corrosive chemicals have been swallowed, the lips may show signs of burning; they may be stained yellow, grey or white and you may notice blisters.

✚ **Consciousness**
Depending on the poison and the quantity taken, the person may be unconscious or may become unconscious at any time.

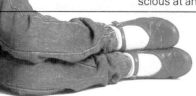

## Action

**1** Call the doctor or ambulance quickly. Tell them what you think the casualty has taken; the person taking the call may tell you what to do while you are waiting.

**2** If the casualty is unconscious, follow the treatment for the unconscious casualty (see page 67) and place her in the *recovery position*.

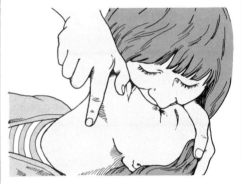

**3** If *mouth-to-mouth* is necessary, be careful not to get any of the poison on your own mouth. If possible wash it off the casualty's face, or use *mouth-to-nose* (see pages 14 to 15).

**4** If the casualty is conscious, watch her carefully because she could lose consciousness.

**5** If the casualty has taken a corrosive poison, give her sips of water or milk to drink.

**6** Transfer the casualty to hospital as soon as possible with any tablets and medicine or containers found near her or any sample of vomit.

# Bites and stings

Most bites and stings cause little more than temporary discomfort. There are some people, however, who are particularly sensitive to the poison or venom injected by a snake or insect so there is a possibility of *shock* if the allergic reaction is severe or there are other complications (see page 25).

## Insect stings

Insects such as bees leave a small sting embedded in the skin which should be removed. Wasp and hornet stings are more alarming than dangerous.

### IMPORTANT

**If a person is stung in the throat, or is unduly sensitive to stings, the throat will swell very quickly and could block the airway and prevent breathing. Give him or her cold water to drink or an ice cube to suck. If breathing becomes difficult, place him or her in the *recovery position* (see page 14). Seek medical aid.**

**Action**

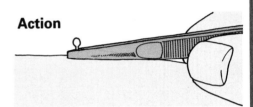

1 If the sting is still in the skin, remove it with a pair of tweezers. Hold the tweezers as close to the skin as possible and pull the sting out. Avoid squeezing the sac at the top of the sting because it will force more poison into the casualty.

2 Apply a *cold compress* to reduce pain and swelling (see page 33).

3 Rest the injured part.

## Weever fish stings

Weever fish are small fish that have sharp poisonous spikes along their backs. They are often found around the coast of Britain and elsewhere, especially in the summer. The spines can become embedded in your foot if you tread on the fish; the foot will swell quickly and be extremely painful.

**Action**

1 Soak the affected foot in a bowl or bucket of water as hot as is comfortable for 15 minutes. This in-activates the poison and will give immediate pain relief.

2 Seek medical aid.

# Snake bites

These are rare in Northern Europe. Adders are the only poisonous snakes native to Britain. They are only slightly poisonous; the bite causes some redness and pain around the bite site. Even in tropical countries where there are many more poisonous snakes, deaths from snake bites are rare.

### Symptoms and signs

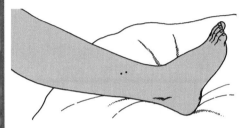

- one or two small puncture marks
- swelling of the affected part.

## IMPORTANT

**Keep the casualty calm and *do not raise the affected limb above the level of the heart.***

**Action**

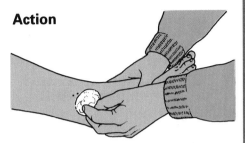

**1** Reassure the casualty. Clean the area around the puncture marks and place a sterile dressing over the area; this also serves to mark the spot.

**2** If the bite is on the hand or upper limb, immobilise the limb with an *arm sling* (see page 56).

**3** If the bite is on the casualty's lower limb, tie her legs together as described for a fractured leg (see pages 46 to 47).

**4** Carry the casualty to a car or wait for the ambulance to take her to hospital. The doctor will then decide whether the casualty needs an anti-venom injection.

# Scorpion stings

Common in hot countries, scorpions are small insects that have long tails with a sting in the end. Scorpion stings are excruciatingly painful but they are unlikely to kill. They can cause *shock* to develop (see page 25).

**Action**
Immobilise the affected part as described for snake bites, above, then seek medical aid. The doctor may give the casualty a local anaesthetic injection to relieve the pain.

# Effects of temperature

To function properly our bodies work best at our normal temperature 36–37°C (97–99°F). To maintain this temperature we adapt to different outside conditions by storing heat when it is cold and by sweating to lose heat when it is hot.

You can help by wearing good-quality warm clothing to keep the heat in when it is cold, and by wearing loose-fitting cotton clothes in hot weather to allow sweat to evaporate. In addition, you should eat high-energy foods when it is cold and drink lots of fluid when it is very hot.

Exposure to extremes of temperature, whether cold or hot, can damage the skin or other body tissues.

## Hypothermia

This is a condition that develops when the body temperature drops below 35°C (95°F). Hypothermia is likely to occur when the temperature is very cold — in wind, rain or snow — and is often seen in adventure training or on expeditions. It is commonly caused by not wearing suitable clothes in cold weather or prolonged immersion in cold water. It can also result from sitting for a long time in a poorly heated or unheated room.

Elderly people and small babies are particularly at risk from hypothermia if the house is not well heated. The symptoms and signs will be the same as those listed around the photograph; however, a baby's face and hands will look bright pink and healthy.

Treat a person with hypothermia as described opposite.

**Symptoms and signs**
Suspect hypothermia if you notice any of the symptoms listed below. If you are on an expedition, stop immediately and treat as described opposite.

+ **Consciousness** If the casualty is not treated quickly, he will collapse and lose consciousness.

+ **Appearance** He will be very pale and shivering badly. His movements may be clumsy and his speech may be slurred.

+ **Behaviour** The person begins to slow down both physically and mentally and may become irritable.

## IMPORTANT

**Never warm the casualty by giving him or her a hot water bottle or an electric blanket.**

**Do not give the casualty any alcohol to drink.**

**Do not encourage the casualty to move around or rub his or her skin to warm up.**

### ✚ Cold
The skin will feel abnormally cold when you touch it.

### Action

**1** *Stop immediately and rest.* Do not continue in the hope that you can find shelter.

**2** Shelter the casualty as much as possible. Wrap him with an emergency blanket and lay him on a groundsheet. If you are a long way from shelter, put a tent up around the casualty if you have one and replace wet clothing with dry clothing. If at home, loosely wrap the casualty in a blanket and warm the room.

**3** Give him a warm drink such as milk or cocoa.

**4** If the casualty loses consciousness, place him in the *recovery position* (see page 18) and keep *checking breathing* (see page 13) and *circulation* (see page 16) and begin *mouth-to-mouth* and *chest compression* if it becomes necessary (see pages 14 to 17).

**5** Look for any signs of frostbite (see overleaf) and treat accordingly.

**6** Arrange to get the casualty to hospital — he must be carried on a stretcher. Do not let him walk.

# Frostbite

This occurs when parts of the body, generally the extremities such as the fingers, toes, ears or chin, become frozen because they are exposed to prolonged or intense cold. Frostbite can be accompanied by hypothermia.

## Symptoms and signs
● prickling pain followed by gradual loss of feeling in the affected area
● skin in affected area will feel hard
● skin becomes mottled blue or sometimes white.

## IMPORTANT

**If possible do not let the casualty walk on a defrosted foot.**

**Never warm the frostbitten part with a hot water bottle.**

## Action

**1** Remove any tight clothing from around the affected part, for example, rings and boots.

**2** Warm the affected part slowly. The casualty can put her hands in her armpits or put her feet in your armpits. Cover her face, nose or ears with dry gloved hands. Keep the affected areas covered until colour and feeling return.

**3** Seek medical aid or call an ambulance.

# Heat exhaustion

Caused by an abnormal loss of salt and water from the body during heavy sweating, heat exhaustion is most common in people who are not used to working in hot climates. It may occur in temperate conditions, for example, in marathons.

## Symptoms and signs
● cramp-like pains and/or headache
● pale, moist skin
● fast, weak pulse
● temperature may be slightly higher than normal (about 38°C/100·5°F).

## Action

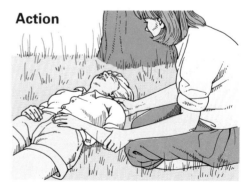

**1** Help the casualty to lie down in a cool place.

# Heatstroke

This is caused by the inability to lose heat from the body by sweating. It is a dangerous condition which occurs wherever it is very hot and humid with no wind. It is most common in tropical countries, although it can also occur in milder climates, particularly in athletes.

## Symptoms and signs
- restlessness
- the casualty may have a headache and feel dizzy
- skin will be flushed and feel very hot
- rapid loss of consciousness
- fast, strong pulse
- body temperature may rise to 40°C (104°F) or higher.

## Action

**1** Lay the casualty down in the coolest place possible and remove his clothes.

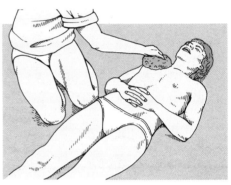

**2** Sponge his body down with cold or tepid water.

**3** Fan his body by hand or with an electric fan.

**4** Get medical aid urgently.

**2** Give her plenty of slightly salted water to drink (¼ teaspoon of salt to a tumbler).

**3** Get medical aid.

# Prickly heat

Common in hot countries, this is an irritating skin condition that results from persistent sweating. To prevent it, avoid excessive exertion and hot drinks when you are not used to the heat. Keep your skin well-ventilated and as dry as possible by wearing loose-fitting cotton clothing.

If prickly heat develops, try taking cold or tepid showers. Do not use any soap and dry yourself very carefully afterwards. You can also dab the affected areas with Calamine lotion to relieve the irritation.

# Small foreign bodies

Foreign bodies in this sense are any small objects — gravel, splinters and so on — that enter the body through a break in the skin or through one of the body's natural openings such as the mouth, nose or ear. Children in particular sometimes swallow small peas or beads or push them into their ears or up their noses.

Loose particles of dirt, in a graze for example, can usually be washed out or removed with clean cotton wool or gauze swabs (see page 26) or with tweezers as shown opposite.

**+ Pain**
The casualty may complain of pain where the splinter went into his hand.

## Splinters

The most common types of foreign body you will come across are very small pieces of wood, glass or metal, which can easily become embedded in the skin. There is always a risk of infection because splinters are rarely clean. If one is still sticking out of the skin, pull it out with tweezers as described opposite. If the end is not visible, let a doctor or nurse remove it because it is very easy to push a splinter further in, making it more difficult to remove later.

## IMPORTANT

**Never dig into the area to get at a small foreign body or splinter.**

**Remember to keep your tetanus inoculations up to date.**

**+ Cause**
Look around you, the
cause of injury may
be near the casualty
as here, for example,
where the wooden
box is near the child.

## Action

**1** Clean the area around the splinter
with soap and water (see *small
cuts and grazes*, page 26).

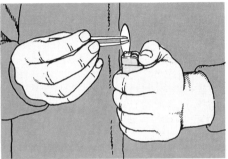

**2** Sterilise a pair of tweezers by
passing them through the flame
from a match or lighter. Allow the
tweezers to cool. Do not wipe the soot
off or touch the ends.

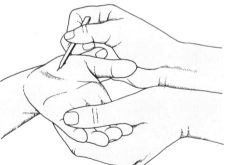

**3** Holding the tweezers as near to
the skin as possible, grasp the end
of the splinter. Pull the splinter out in
the opposite direction to that in which it
entered the skin.

**4** If the splinter breaks, do not
continue. Seek medical aid; anti-
tetanus inoculation may be necessary.

# Foreign body in the eye

The most common foreign bodies found in eyes are pieces of grit or dust, eyelashes or small insects.

## Action

**1** Tell the casualty to try not to rub her eye.

**2** Ask the casualty to sit down in a chair facing a light and to lean back slightly. Wash your hands.

**3** Ask the casualty to look up, stand behind her and supporting her chin with one hand, gently draw the lower lid down and outward.

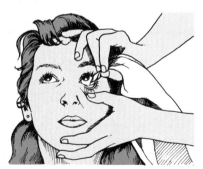

**4** If you can see the object on the eyelid or the white part of the eye, lift it off with a moistened wisp of cotton wool or the corner of a *clean* handkerchief or paper tissue.

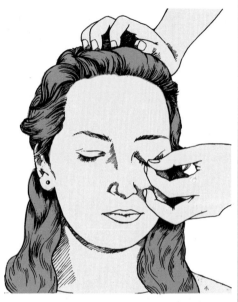

**5** If you think the particle is on the upper lid, ask the casualty to look down, grasp the upper lid by the lashes with your finger and thumb and draw it down and out over the lower lid.

**6** If you have not been successful, help her put her eye under water and tell her to blink — the particle should float off.

**7** If you cannot remove the object, seek medical aid.

## IMPORTANT

**Never try to remove anything that is on the coloured part of the eye or that is stuck in the eye. Cover the eye with a sterile eye dressing and take the casualty to hospital.**

# Foreign body in the ear

This is most common in young children who have a habit of putting things into their ears. Occasionally insects get into a person's ear.

**IMPORTANT**

Never try to dig anything out of the ear or nose.

**Action**

**1** Reassure the casualty.

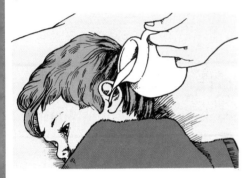

**2** If an insect is in his ear, help him to lie down on his side with the affected ear uppermost, and gently pour tepid water into the ear. The insect should float to the surface.

**3** If a child has pushed something into his ear, tilt his head so that the affected ear is downward; the object may drop out.

**4** If you cannot get the object or insect out easily, seek medical aid as soon as possible.

# Foreign body in the nose

Again this is most common with children trying to put things in their noses.

**Action**

**1** Reassure the casualty and tell her to breathe through her mouth.

**2** Take her to hospital as quickly as possible.

# Foreign body in the throat

If a particle of food or a small object is lodged in a person's throat, he or she may choke (see page 20). If a casualty has a fishbone stuck in his or her throat, *do not try to do anything*. Reassure the casualty and seek medical aid.

# Transporting the injured

When moving a casualty, his or her safety and well-being should be your first consideration. Never move anyone who is seriously injured unless there is immediate danger to life; wait for skilled help to arrive. If you have to move the casualty, immobilise the joints above and below any suspected fracture (see pages 42 to 57) or other serious injury before you do so.

There are various ways to move someone; the method you use will depend on the injury, the number of people available to help, the casualty's build and the distance and route to be travelled. Stretchers are always used to carry a seriously ill or injured person. The standard stretcher shown below is the one you are most likely to use.

## Standard stretchers

When closed the poles lie close to-gether with the canvas bed folded down and held in position by two straps. To open the stretcher, place it on its side with the runners facing you and the studs or buckles on the straps uppermost; undo the straps. Pull

the top pole up, very carefully kick the traverses open with your heel and lay the stretcher on its runners.

## Principles of lifting

If you follow these rules carefully you will find yourself able to lift fairly heavy objects without undue strain. *Do not practise lifting anything or anyone heavier than yourself and never try to move a person by yourself if there are people available to help.*
● stand with your feet slightly apart to maintain a stable, balanced posture
● keep your back straight; bend at the knees if necessary
● use the most powerful muscles in your body – your thighs, hips and shoulders – to take as much of the weight as possible
● keep the weight as close to your body as possible.

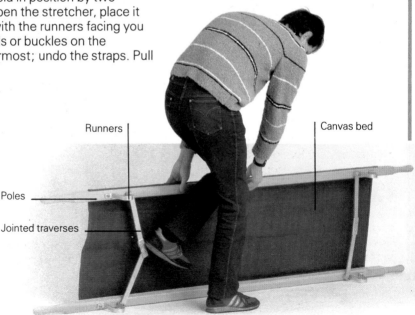

Runners

Canvas bed

Poles

Jointed traverses

# Moving a casualty to safety

If danger makes it necessary to move a casualty, approach her from behind and fold one of her arms across her chest (use an uninjured arm). Slide your arms beneath her armpits and grasp her arm. If possible, get a bystander to steady her head and keep it in line with her neck and chest, then move slowly backward dragging the casualty with you keeping her body in a straight line.

# Carrying light casualties

There are two ways of carrying injured children and lightweight people; you can cradle them in your arms or carry them pick-a-back fashion.
**Cradle method** Pass one arm under the casualty's thighs and the other around his or her back and lift.
**Pick-a-back** Squat down with your back to the casualty and put his or her arms around your neck. Put your arms around his or her legs and stand up.

# Helping a casualty to walk

Known as the *human crutch*, this method is used to help support a slightly injured casualty who is able to walk. Stand at the casualty's injured side and put the arm nearest you around your neck and hold on to her hand. Put your other arm around her waist and grasp the clothing at her hip. If the casualty needs more support, give her a walking stick or ask another person to help support her other side.

## IMPORTANT

**Never use this method if an upper limb is injured.**

# Four-handed seat

This method requires two people and is used to carry a person who cannot walk but who can use her arms for support.

Stand behind the casualty facing your helper. To make the seat, each of you should grasp your own left wrist with your right hand and each other's right wrist with the free hand (see below). Ask the casualty to steady herself by putting an arm around each of you as shown below and to sit back on to your hands (see right). Rise gently, taking the casualty's weight, and set off, both leading with your outside feet.

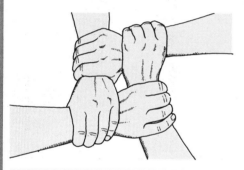

# Chair support

If you have to move a casualty along a narrow passage or up or down stairs, you can sit him or her in a chair and carry the chair with another first aider. Before you start, make sure the chair can take the casualty's weight and clear any obstructions or loose mats out of the way. For additional safety, secure the casualty to the chair by tying *broad-fold bandages* (see page 40) around the chair and the casualty before you lift him or her.

**1** Sit the casualty in a chair. Stand behind the chair, with your helper standing in front of it, facing the casualty. Both check that she is well back in the chair and is comfortably supported before lifting her.

# Two-handed seat

This is another method for two first aiders which can be used when a casualty has a chest or upper limb injury and cannot support herself.

Squat down, facing each other, one on each side of the casualty and each pass an arm around his back and grasp clothing on the side farthest from you. Pass your free hands under the casualty's thighs and grasp each other's wrists (see below). Working together, gently raise the casualty and set off, both leading with your outside feet taking normal paces.

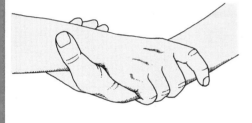

**2** Support the back of the chair and the casualty while your helper holds the front legs. Working together, tilt the chair back slightly and lift it. With the casualty facing forward, move along the passage.

### Lifting a wheelchair-bound person

This can be done without lifting the person out of the chair by adapting the chair support method. Secure the brakes — ask the person where these are if you cannot find them. Make sure he or she is sitting well back in the chair and, standing on one side of the chair with your helper facing you on the other side, both lift the wheelchair by *holding the fixed parts and never the wheels*. Note that the arm rests and side supports are often removable.

# Preparing a stretcher

To make a casualty feel comfortable and secure on a stretcher, place a blanket on it as shown below and wrap it around him or her.

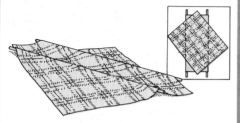

**1** Place the blanket diagonally over the stretcher so that opposite corners are at either end of the stretcher bed.

**2** Place the casualty on the stretcher (see opposite). Bring the bottom point up over her feet and tuck a small fold between her ankles.

**3** Fold the top point in around the casualty's head and neck.

**4** Bring the righthand side of the blanket over her and tuck her in. Repeat on the other side.

# Loading a stretcher

A minimum of four people will always be needed to load a stretcher and one person should take charge to make sure everyone moves together. If possible, use a blanket to move the casualty. Check that the blanket can take the casualty's weight before you start: one person should lie on the blanket while two others try to lift it.

## Placing a blanket under a casualty

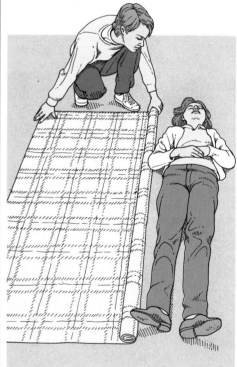

**1** Roll a blanket lengthwise for half its width and place it on the ground beside the casualty with the roll up against her injured side (or most seriously injured side). If she is conscious, explain the procedure.

**2** All four first aiders should kneel alongside the casualty level with her head, shoulders, thighs and feet. Working together, turn her towards you, then move the rolled part of the blanket up against her back.

**3** Gently roll her back on to the blanket over the top of the roll and enough over on to her other side to enable you to unroll part of the blanket, then turn her on to her back again.

## Blanket lift

Place the stretcher in line with the casualty's body as close to her head as possible. Firmly roll both sides of the blanket up to her sides. Two people should stand opposite each other on either side of the casualty level with her shoulders and the other two should stand level with her knees. Squat down and grasp the blanket with the palms of your hands downward and fingers on the inside of the rolled edge. The two first aiders at the casualty's head should have one hand level with her head and the other level with her waist, the other two should have one hand near her hips and the other level with her ankles. Working together, lift the casualty high enough for someone else to slide the stretcher underneath, then gently lower her in place.

# Appendix

This section of the book includes Holger Nielsen, an alternative method for getting air into the lungs of a casualty who is not breathing, together with information about first aid equipment and how to store it.

## Holger Nielsen ventilation

This method of ventilation was not included in the *Breathing* chapter (see pages 10 to 21) because it should be used only as a last resort when *mouth-to-mouth* (see page 14) is impossible, for example, if the casualty is trapped face down or when the face is too badly injured. Holger Nielsen is not as effective as *mouth-to-mouth* as it introduces less than half the amount of air into the casualty's lungs and it is impossible to carry out *external chest compression* (see page 16) with the casualty lying face down.

### Method

**1** Lay the casualty face down and turn his head to one side. Open his mouth and pull the tongue forward to open the airway. Sweep your finger round inside the mouth to remove any foreign matter.

**2** If the casualty is still not breathing, bring his arms above his head, bend them at the elbows and, resting one hand on the other, put the hands underneath the upper part of the casualty's cheek.

**3** Kneel on one knee at the casualty's head with your knee close to his forehead and your other foot near his elbow.

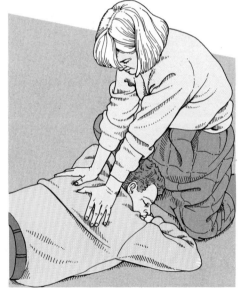

**4** Place the heels of your hands over the casualty's shoulder blades level with his armpits; put your thumbs along either side of his spine and spread your fingers out over the casualty's rib cage.

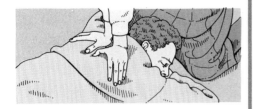

**5** Keeping your arms straight, rock forward steadily until they are vertical; this compresses the chest, corresponding to breathing out.

**6** Begin to rock backwards and immediately slip your hands towards the casualty's armpits, along the arms as far as the elbows and grasp the casualty's elbows.

**7** Still moving backward raise the casualty's elbows until you are vertical and can feel resistance from his shoulders. This expands the chest and corresponds to breathing in.

**8** Move your hands back to the shoulder blades and repeat the cycle of movements, working rhythmically and taking about five seconds to complete each cycle.

# First aid equipment

Although we have told you how to improvise dressings in an emergency, it is much better to keep a selection of the dressings and bandages recommended throughout the book handy at home and/or in your car. You should have several different sized sterile dressings (see page 27); an assortment of adhesive dressings (see page 27); a triangular bandage; a few 25g (1oz) rolls of cotton wool; a packet of antiseptic wipes; a couple of crepe and/or conforming bandages (see page 64); a selection of safety pins; tweezers and a pair of blunt-ended scissors.

All the equipment should be kept in a clean, dry airtight box. Label the box clearly so that it is easily identifiable and keep it in a dry place, not the bathroom where it could be affected by steam.

**Storing triangular bandages**
Triangular bandages can be used several times and should be kept neatly folded when not in use. Make a *narrow-fold bandage* (see page 40). Turn the ends of the bandage in to meet in the middle of the bandage (A). Continue folding the ends into the middle until it is the right size to fit in your box (B).

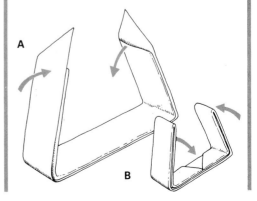

A

B

# Index

## A

## B

## C

## D

## E

## F

*0496 2310*

# Acknowledgments

**Project editor** Jemima Dunne

**Designers** Carole Ash, Frances de Rees

**Managing editor** Daphne Razazan
**Art editor** Anne-Marie Bulat

**Photography** Paul Fletcher

**Typesetting** Cambrian Typesetters

**Reproduction** A. Mondadori